BATHROOM REMODELING
HANDBOOK

By the Editors of Sunset and Southern Living

Period decor and modern convenience: this remodeled bathroom combines nostalgic new fixtures with genuine antiques. Design: Diane Johnson Design.

Acknowledgments

Our thanks to the many professionals who generously shared their expertise with us—particularly L. E. Olstead of L. E. Wentz, General Contractors; Stanley M. Macey, CKD, instructor, Cañada College; American Standard Plumbing Products Division; John F. Dahl Plumbing, Heating & Air Conditioning; Mac and Lou Construction Co.; and Pacific Gas & Electric.

Coordinating Editor:
Cornelia Fogle

Photo Editor:
Scott Fitzgerrell

Research & Text:
Susan E. Schlangen
Bob T. Martin

Contributing Editor:
Cynthia Overbeck Bix

Technical Editor:
Don Rutherford

Photo Stylist:
JoAnn Masaoka

Design:
Joe di Chiarro

Illustrations:
Bill Oetinger
Mark Pechenik

Photographers: Edward Bigelow: 76 right, 77 right, 78 bottom. **Jack McDowell:** 2 right, 5, 6, 7, 8, 9, 10, 12, 13, 50, 51, 61 top & bottom right, 64, 66 top, 68 top left, 71 top, 75 top, 77 bottom left, 79 top. **Stephen Marley:** 3, 61 left, 78 top. **Rob Super:** 14, 54, 56 right, 63 top. **Tom Wyatt:** 1, 11, 15, 16, 49, 55, 56 left, 57, 58 top, 59, 60, 62, 63 bottom, 65, 66 bottom, 68 top right, 69, 70 top, 72, 73, 74, 75 bottom, 76 left, 77 top, 79 bottom, 80. **Tom Yee:** 2 left, 52, 53, 58 bottom, 67, 68 bottom, 70 bottom, 71 bottom.

Cover: Remodeled bathroom combines a sunny skylight with light-colored walls, tile, laminate cabinets, and synthetic marble countertop. Bright brass hardware sparkles against a white sink and matching platform tub. Design: Rick Waxman. Photographed by Glenn Christiansen. Cover designed by Lynne B. Morrall.

Editor: Elizabeth L. Hogan

Tenth printing May 1992

Balcony bathroom looks out on the sea and sky through a generous skylight; the master bedroom lies below. The large, tile-topped mahogany counter features double basins and maximum storage. Architects: MLA/Architects.

Sophisticated master bath is tall, dark, and handsome in its suit of matte-finish tile and black plastic laminate. Design: William Conti.

Contents

Fanlight above and mirror below keep things light and lively in an expanded second-floor bathroom. Heavy moldings add a traditional flavor to a scheme that's really modern in both concept and execution. Architect: Robert Peterson.

BATHROOM MAKEOVERS

Eight case histories · From facelifts to total transformations

Nothing is more helpful when you're first considering a remodeling project than to consult the experience of others. That's why we've chosen to begin this book with a series of factual accounts. Starting on page 6, you'll find eight full-color examples of successful bathroom remodeling. Projects range from moderate facelifts to several quite complete—and almost magical—transformations. Along the way you're likely to find at least one that will pique your curiosity, fire your imagination, and, ideally, resemble the situation you face in planning or remodeling your own bathroom.

The following chapters lead you step by step through the design and remodeling process. "Planning Guidelines" (page 16) explores the design decisions you'll face, examines basic bathroom layouts, and includes a section on products and materials currently available. "Design Ideas" (page 48) contains more than 50 color photographs covering everything from open plans to storage details.

Finally, "Remodeling Basics" (page 80) shows you in words and pictures how to dismantle and install everything from fixtures and fittings to surfacing materials and storage units. There's additional information on lighting fixtures, as well as overviews of your structural, plumbing, heating, ventilating, and electrical systems. Special features throughout the book discuss personalized bathrooms, safety, energy conservation, painting techniques, and greenhouse windows.

The book follows the logical progression of a bathroom remodeling project and is divided into sections for easy reference. To begin, though, it's fun—and instructive—to see what others have done. Simply turn the page.

The case of the unwanted wall

When this bathroom was turned over to a teenager, the time was ripe for a much-needed overhaul. Since only one person would use the room, the privacy of separate compartments was no longer necessary. Uniting the two small spaces became a primary goal of the remodeling effort. Further dramatic improvement came with the addition of a skylight; everything else was basically cosmetic.

In the newly combined space, tile and cedar surfaces replace the drab originals. A new glass shower enclosure and step-down tile tub present minimal barriers to the light and to the eye. Though not enlarged, the bathroom now offers an entirely different, more inviting ambience. The refreshing color scheme sets woody browns and sparkling brass against clean whites; the skylight and its attendant track lights provide around-the-clock illumination. There's even a stereo system—after all, the bathroom was remodeled for a teenager.

Design: Rick Sambol.

Bright new interior (left) was achieved with minimal fuss. The partition wall was removed, "decompartmentalizing" the original bath (above). All fixtures were replaced, but their locations remain the same. A new skylight brings light into the formerly dark space; its effect is enhanced by a large mirror and by the light finishes used on most walls. Brass tones and the complementary browns of the cedar cabinet, the cedar wall opposite (reflected in the mirror), and the tile floor and fixtures stand out boldly against the white.

Space shuffle

This master bathroom was remodeled in conjunction with a master bedroom addition. It's a good example of how existing spaces can be revised and consolidated to produce something quite different—even marvelous—out of seemingly hopeless raw material.

Adding the bedroom created a different set of priorities in the adjacent spaces: the original bedroom became a sitting room, which made the old dressing area largely unnecessary—in fact, redundant. The dressing area could now be incorporated into a new bathroom plan. With this decided, it was a simple conceptual step (and not too difficult physically) to tear out the wall dividing the dressing area from the bathroom and design a single gracious space with luxuriously roomy tub, a long counter with two sinks, and lots of storage in the cabinets and shelves. The old tub and toilet compartment was reduced in size; now just a toilet compartment, it retains its privacy.

The original bathroom was dim and dark, so lighting was a major item on the remodeling agenda. A large plate glass window illuminates the tub area, and a room-length skylight with diffusing panel highlights the ceiling treatment. A wall-size mirror, white tile, and off-white cabinets bounce light around the room. The ceiling and storage wall are of warm-toned redwood; the tile grout was tinted to match the wood. Tub and toilet areas share a view of an attractive private garden added just outside the bathroom.

Architect: William A. Churchill.

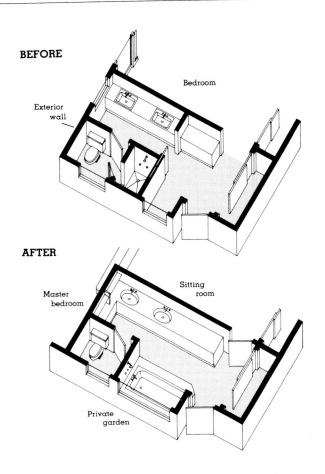

BEFORE

Exterior wall

Bedroom

AFTER

Master bedroom

Sitting room

Private garden

Mirrored wall seems to double the size of the completely remodeled bathroom (left). The formerly dark and dreary space (above) is now filled with light from a skylight and the large new window (see facing page). A tiled wall at left divides the toilet compartment from the rest of the bath. New laminate cabinets and natural-wood shelves offer greatly expanded storage space.

Bathing in the lap of luxury is a reality, thanks to the new tub with its generous, light-gathering window and view of a small private garden beyond. A mini-blind drops down when more privacy is desired or when the sun becomes too intense.

Darkness at noon

In its original form, this bathroom had many of the problems typical of baths on the north side of a house. Even at noon it was a dank little cave, dimly lit by a small, north-facing window. Mildew was always poised to strike whenever the owners relaxed their vigilance. As they mapped out a new, larger plan, remodeling for daylight became an important concern—in addition to the welcome light, the sun's heat would help to keep the room dry.

Now, daylight floods in through two skylights. A raised ceiling, light finishes, and a wall-size mirror spread light and warmth around the room. The bathroom also grew by taking 2½ feet from the master bedroom. This made room for a second basin and a wider tub; an unneeded door was eliminated.

Architect: Weston Whitfield.

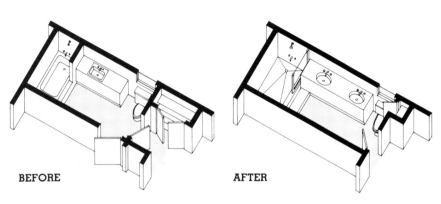

BEFORE

AFTER

New doorway and wall annex part of the master bedroom beyond. The open plan places the toilet and a new linen cabinet at one end of the room.

Skylights in a raised ceiling illuminate the north-facing bathroom (left). Warm, light colors and a large expanse of mirror help balance the sunlight and ban mildew; tile color matches the sinks for an integrated look. Photo below shows the bath in the midst of an earlier facelift; even with a large mirror, lighting was a problem and the space was damp and uninviting.

Unification project

Two pocket-size baths were the basis of this ingeniously remodeled bathroom. Each of the tiny spaces was plagued by the same problems: too many fixtures in too little space, and floorplans that made them hard to use—or even to walk through.

The solution was to combine them, eliminating half the fixtures and doors. Moving a partition wall 3 feet into a neighboring room increased space. In the new bathroom, one shower was retained; the other became a compact laundry center. An oval vanity stands just out of traffic at the junction of the two original rooms, flanked by a pocket door that allows use of the bathroom by two people. The toilet was moved to the area vacated by one of the sinks, with a new, larger window placed above it.

Design: Osburn Design.

BEFORE **AFTER**

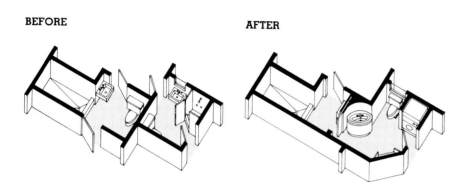

New laundry center hides behind accordion shade and replaces a shower made redundant when spaces were combined. The display and storage niche is part of an angled wall that borrows space from the adjacent room. New cork flooring picks up the tones of the wood.

Forest green shower and sink provide color accents in this fir-clad bathroom with period touches. A large, functional mirror "opens" the shower wall. Though two baths were combined, the room is still small, and everything is compact in scale. Photo below shows one of the cramped original baths; the doorway is one of two that were walled off to improve efficiency.

Open-plan elegance

To call the original bathroom "stark" would be a kindness; it was not a space designed to be enjoyed. The 5 by 8-foot room was poorly planned and barely functional. Storage and lighting, for example, were virtually ignored. The master bedroom it served also needed improvement; in particular, its closet, located squarely inside the doorway, was an awkward eyesore.

The breakthrough idea in this owner-designed remodeling project was a 5-foot-wide "pop out" of the exterior bedroom and bathroom walls. In the bedroom this added space was used for a new wardrobe/dressing room, and the offending closet was torn out. In the bathroom, the space became a skylit bay that's the key to a truly magical transformation of humdrum raw material into a tranquil retreat of exceptional beauty.

The bay is sized to accommodate a standard 4 by 6-foot double-dome skylight. Beneath the skylight, a site-built tub/shower sits on a new concrete foundation. The toilet now occupies the space of a former closet, which was closed off from the hallway and annexed to the bathroom. The old toilet niche became a large linen closet.

Dove gray tile and paint give the newly enlarged space an airy coolness. A local cabinetmaker provided beautiful walnut cabinetry that adds a distinctive accent of richness—an appropriate touch in a bathroom that's always on view as a part of the new master bedroom suite.

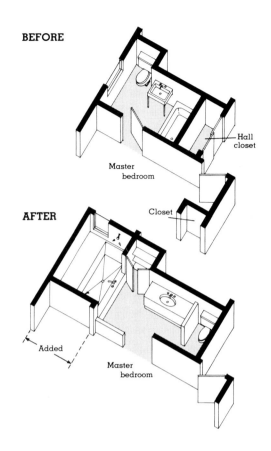

BEFORE

Hall closet

Master bedroom

AFTER

Closet

Added

Master bedroom

Bare function, with the accent on "bare," characterized the original bath. Angle of view shown above matches that on the facing page.

Bathroom expanded inward, taking over an adjacent hallway closet that became the new toilet niche. The closet's back wall is now a divider between the toilet and vanity areas; the original tub stood just inside this wall. Walnut cabinets are well protected by marine varnish; brass fixtures complement the wood's rich, dark tones. Generous mirrors help enlarge the space even more.

Serene composition of cool gray tile and darkly luminous walnut shines softly in an open-plan bathroom that's now visible from the master bedroom (reflected in the ceiling-height mirror). The new tub/shower sits under a large skylight in a "popped-out" bay. The louvered door seen in the mirror leads to a wardrobe/dressing room—a continuation of the bay. Existing exterior and partition walls were opened to provide easy access and to allow light from the skylight to flow into both rooms. A linen closet with doors of bookmatched walnut occupies the former toilet niche.

Sleek lines, soft curves

Smooth, curving lines and "eased edges" distinguish this radically transformed bathroom, clad in an almost reptilian skin of flawlessly laid mosaic tile.

Outmoded and too small, the bath had been overdue for a change. The original plan measured just 7 by 8 feet, so the first order of business was to enlarge the space; since other rooms hemmed the bathroom in on three sides, the only way to go was out. A 4 by 14-foot shedlike addition neatly doubles the square footage, providing room for a relocated toilet and curvilinear tub-shower; it also frees space for a second sink and extra cabinets with greatly increased storage (see plans). The ceiling was raised to the roofline, where a skylight handles daylighting chores—windows had to be small because of neighbors' proximity.

Design: Rick Sambol for Kitchen Craft of Marin.

BEFORE

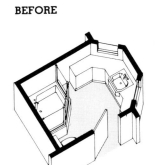

AFTER

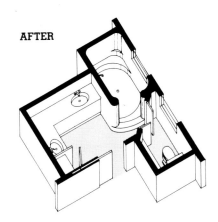

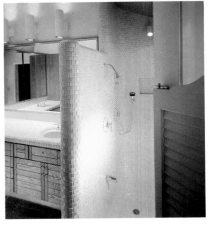

Curtainless tub/shower combination stands outside the original exterior wall, which became a partial divider between the shower and the rest of the bathroom.

Inside the bathroom, everything has changed (left). Before, space was tight, storage inconvenient, and clutter inevitable (below). The new design features clean lines, curved edges, and lots of storage—including ample medicine cabinets behind the sliding mirror.

Architectural legerdemain

Magic is easy to understand once the trick's explained. This one operates on something akin to the domino principle; look carefully at the plans.

First a narrow atrium was incorporated into the nearby guest bath, enabling the master bath to be reoriented and enlarged. Then traffic flow was redirected: unlike the original plan that led the owners on a serpentine path, the new one avoids dividing the bedroom wall and improves bathroom access at the same time.

The new master bath borrows space from the old guest bath, and a step-down tub/shower now sits behind a low divider in a glassy bay added outside the original foundation. A skylight shines above. Space is nearly tripled and storage more than doubled.

Architect: MLA/Architects.

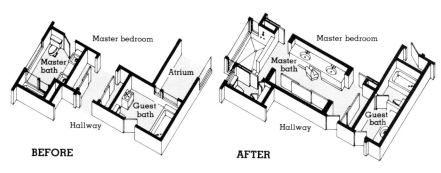

BEFORE

AFTER

Original bathroom was small, with little storage and poorly balanced light. The view from the door showed typical '50s appointments.

New master bath was reoriented 90 degrees from the original (see plans). The long, mirror-lined room features voluminous storage in the counter cabinets at right and the full-length wardrobe at left. The original exterior wall, reduced to half height, now separates the room from an added tub/shower beyond; space was also widened by approximately the counter's width.

Open-plan master bathroom, part of a second-floor addition, makes good use of natural light. The overall scheme combines generous space and luxurious appointments with a distinctly Southwestern style. (For a better view of the tub, see page 69.) Design: Diane Johnson Design.

PLANNING GUIDELINES

Decision making · Design · Floor plans · Products

The hallmark of today's bathrooms is style; it can be found in elegant powder rooms, gracious guest baths, efficient family bathrooms, and spacious master suites. Inspired by innovative designs, fashionable fixtures and fittings, and a refreshing palette of colors, the zest for home decorating has progressed to the bathroom from other parts of the house. The introduction of new products and materials—stylish yet durable—has added momentum.

But changes in lifestyle and the economy are at the heart of the bathroom remodeling trend. More and more people are deciding to make the most of the home they already own, rather than move on to another one. And in the process they're changing the face of the bathroom. Not long ago, the standard bath was simply a room with utilitarian fixtures. Today's bathroom serves many needs. At its best, it can be a sanctuary from the busy world and a place to pamper yourself.

Planning your new bathroom can be one of the most enjoyable aspects of remodeling; it's the first step toward creating the kind of room you want. In this chapter, you'll learn about bathroom planning, from evaluating your existing bathroom to drawing floor plans for a new one, and determining the best ways to launch your project. The varied choices in fixtures, fittings, and materials are discussed in the "Bathroom showcase" (pages 31–40).

The key to planning is to define your needs and preferences, then adapt them to your home and budget. Consider realistically what work you can and can't do yourself, then use professional help as needed to bring your bathroom project to completion.

Your present plan

"Where do I start?" is one of the most-asked questions about remodeling. Here's the answer: Begin with an inventory of your existing bathroom. Once you've assessed the room's current conditions and developed some remodeling goals, it will be easier to uncover the room's potential for greater comfort, more convenience, and better appearance. If you envision extensive remodeling, measure the room and draw it to scale (see pages 20–21); you'll use this drawing as a basis for planning and designing your bathroom.

If you want, you can arrange to have an architect or designer work with you to establish goals and draw the existing floor plan. For information on working with professionals, see pages 42–44.

BATHROOM INVENTORY

If you're like most people, you seldom take a critical look at a room—you simply know that you feel at ease in some rooms and uncomfortable in others. To analyze your reaction to your present bathroom, take the bathroom inventory—one of the most important tools in designing your new bathroom. It's a fact-finding process in which you identify specific conditions you'd like to improve, evaluate strengths and weaknesses, and set goals for remodeling.

Begin by casting a critical eye on your bathroom's appearance. When you enter the room, consider the overall impression it makes. Would this room be an asset if you were selling your house? Do you see chipped fixtures or caulkless cracks? What features are distracting or unattractive? The look of a room can be spoiled by a busy wallpaper or something as simple as clutter—too many towels on too few bars or excessive sink-side paraphernalia.

Trends come and go, and the bathroom is not immune to changing fashion. Maybe it's time to pull the plug on outdated surface treatments, colors, or accessories. You may or may not decide to replace fixtures or tile; sometimes a simple redecorating can be a surprisingly effective and inexpensive way to update a room's appearance.

First, look at the surfaces. Would the bathroom's style improve if you resurfaced the walls, floor, ceiling, countertops, or cabinetry? Are your doors and drawers ready for new hardware? Would new windows, tub, or shower doors improve the room?

But don't stop when you've examined these relatively superficial elements. Move on to the fundamentals of the room and everything in it—and the way it all works (or fails to work) for the people who use it.

Layout. In a small room such as a bathroom, layout is especially important. Generally, the term refers to the location of fixtures and the space between them. It also refers to the location of doors and windows, as well as storage areas for towels, bathroom tissue, grooming aids, cosmetics, and cleaning supplies. When two or more people use the bathroom at the same time, layout related problems become more apparent.

Consider the following questions in relation to your bathroom's layout: Does the door open into the room? If so, can it inconvenience someone inside? When open, do cabinet or vanity doors and drawers block the door? Can two people use the sink or vanity area at the same time? Would your family benefit from the added privacy of a compartmentalized bathroom, with tub, shower, or toilet separate from each other and from the vanity? Is there ample room for toweling dry without hitting elbows? Is the bathroom tissue within easy reach?

Fixtures & fittings. Before you rush out to buy new fixtures and fittings, consider whether or not the existing ones can be cleaned, refinished, or repaired. If not, let your experience with them guide you in your choice of replacements. Decide what features you like and dislike about your current equipment. Are you pleased with the sizes, shapes, and materials? Are the faucets easy to turn on and off? Can you adjust water temperature as easily as you'd like? Are you content with a center-set faucet, or would you like a single-control one? For more information about fixtures and fittings, see pages 32 and 34–37.

Walls, floor & ceiling. Moisture is the enemy of most room surfaces and their subsurfaces. Water warps flooring, deteriorates paint, and wilts wallpaper. Examine these bathroom surfaces for chips, cracks, bubbles, mold, mildew, and other maladies. Are the grout and caulking in good condition?

If any of these surfaces are damaged or you want to make a decorative change, be sure to consider moisture-resistance when you choose new materials.

Paint used in bathrooms should be washable and resistant to mildew as well as to moisture—a gloss or semigloss enamel paint is recommended. If you prefer wallpaper, it too should be washable and should be applied with a moisture-resistant or waterproof adhesive as recommended by the manufacturer. Nonporous wall coverings, either sprayed with a thin coat of vinyl or made of solid vinyl backed with paper or fabric, are a good choice. Solid vinyls are hard-wearing, scrubbable, and stain-resistant; vinyl-coated wallpapers are washable, but aren't particularly durable. Both come in a variety of colors, patterns, and textures.

For floors, resilient sheets and tiles are a good choice because they're flexible, easy to install, and resistant to moisture and stains. You can choose from many colors, patterns, textures, and styles. See page 40 for more information about materials commonly used in the bathroom and in the manufacture of fixtures.

Countertops. Do you have ample counter space in your bathroom? If not, decide where you need more room for storage or display, or simply for a convenient place to put things down. Do you need additional space near the sink? Are existing countertops in good condition? Are joints and corners easy to keep clean? Would you prefer a different type of countertop material, or has the present material been just right?

Storage. Before you plan to increase your storage capacity, clean out and organize existing storage areas—sometimes better organization goes a long way toward solving the problem of insufficient storage. If you're still short of space, determine your most pressing storage needs: Do you need shelves, drawers, cabinets, or bins? Would you like a recessed medicine cabinet, overhead storage for cleaning supplies, or a tilt-out bin to hold your bathroom scale?

For more serious storage needs, consider adding a vanity or other kinds of cabinets, available in matching modular units with shelves and bins. You can also rearrange the layout, build a closet in the room, or even enlarge the room to gain space.

Lighting. Old bathrooms rarely have enough properly placed lights. If your bathroom has only one overhead light or a single light above the medicine cabinet, you'll certainly want to give some thought to improving the room's artificial lighting, and perhaps the natural light as well.

Would you like to add a skylight or enlarge a window? Do both general and task lighting need upgrading? Are you pleased with the appearance of existing light fixtures, and is the kind of light (fluorescent or incandescent) what you want?

Electrical outlets & switches. Note the location and number of electrical outlets and switches; consider whether you want to change their location or number. If you need more electrical outlets, you might want to replace a single outlet with a double one. For greater convenience, you can install two and three-way switches for lights.

Heating & ventilation. A controlled temperature and good ventilation are basic for bathroom comfort. No one enjoys the shock of a chilly bathroom on a cold morning. In a poorly ventilated bathroom, you may gasp for air in the middle of a steamy shower or have to stop to wipe off a foggy mirror while shaving. Note any problems caused by poor heating or ventilation—don't overlook the problem of mold or mildew. To achieve the comfort you want, you can purchase a ventilation fan or electric space heater—both are fairly easy to install.

Water & energy conservation. It's easy for a conscientious remodeler to avoid wasting these two resources and save money at the same time (see page 41). Heating the bathroom and heating water consume a lot of energy. Are the water heater, pipes, and walls well insulated? Is the shower head equipped with a flow restrictor or shut-off valve? If you plan to buy a new toilet, have you considered a water-saving model?

Privacy. Does the door or window of your bathroom open to a public area? If so, you may want to consider relocating the opening or developing special window or exterior treatments to improve the privacy. You should also check your bathroom for uninsulated pipes; insufficient floor, wall, and ceiling insulation; and finishing materials that reflect sound.

Accessories. List your bathroom accessories and note any additions or deletions you'd like to make, as well as changes you want in quality, quantity, or style. Would you like to replace mismatched accessories with a coordinated collection in glass, ceramic, or brightly colored plastic? Consider the material or finish of each accessory. Do you want the finish on towel bars, mirror frames, and cabinet hardware to match existing or new fittings? Also look at your towels; aside from being functional, do they accent or complement the room's color scheme?

Maintenance. Some bathrooms are easier to maintain than others. Evaluate the trouble spots in your bathroom, such as soap buildup, discolored grout, and streaked walls. In planning your project, consider installing smooth, seamless or jointless materials (such as synthetic marble) and ones especially designed to withstand moisture. If your fixtures are difficult to clean, you may want to refinish or replace them.

Family needs. A bathroom should be easy for everyone to use. Take time to consider the special needs of family members and regular visitors, including children and elderly or handicapped persons. Can an adult bathe a child safely and comfortably? Is the tub or shower equipped with a nonskid base and grab bars? If wheelchair access is a consideration, is the entry wide enough, and is there ample space for easy turning? Can all the fixtures be used without assistance? If you're remodeling exclusively for a handicapped person, you should consult early in your planning with an architect or designer who has experience in this area.

Setting goals for remodeling

If you've conducted a thorough inventory, you now have a number of ideas to incorporate into your remodeling plans. To decide on your primary goals, review the inventory and list all the improvements you'd like to make in order of importance.

To make it easier to establish priorities, you can assign a numerical rating to each improvement, or designate each as "must do" or "would like to do." The finished list will keep your remodeling goals in focus and guide you in setting a budget, working with professionals, and selecting products and materials.

(Continued on next page)

. . . Your present plan

DRAW YOUR EXISTING PLAN

You've taken a critical look at your bathroom, analyzing its good points and noting areas that you want to improve. If your goals point to redecorating or minor remodeling, skip ahead to the design section (pages 22–30) or the "Bathroom showcase" (pages 31–40) for specifics that apply to your situation.

For more ambitious remodeling plans, you'll need to measure and draw the room to scale. These drawings of an existing floor plan and elevations (the wall areas) can help you in several ways:

• To increase your awareness of the room's dimensions and space.

• To serve as a basis for drawing your new floor plan (you'll lay tracing paper over the existing plan, trace elements you want to keep, and add new ones).

• To detail information for designers, architects, or contractors.

• To provide documentation for a building permit. Depending on the extent of your remodeling, you may have to submit an existing floor plan with the proposed alterations to the building department before a permit can be issued.

The following guidelines tell you how to measure your bathroom, record those measurements, and draw a two-dimensional floor plan to scale. You'll also learn how to draw elevations to scale.

Measuring the room

Before you begin to measure, draw a rough sketch of the bathroom, its elements, and any adjacent areas that may be included in the remodeling. Make the sketch as large as the paper allows, so you'll have ample room to write in the dimensions. You can represent walls and partitions with a thick single line (as shown on the floor plan on the facing page). Note any suspected deviations from the standard wall and partition thickness (usually about 5 inches). The sketch should also show all projections, recesses, windows, doors, and doorswings.

Tools. Listed below are some tools and supplies that will help you with your measuring and drawing. You can find them at hardware, stationery, and art supply stores. The architect's scale converts actual measurements to scale measurements, and vice versa.

• Steel rule
• Ruler
• Compass
• Tracing paper
• Masking tape
• Pencils and eraser
• Architect's template
• Architect's scale
• Graph paper (scale: 4 squares per inch)
• Clipboard or pad with 8½ by 11-inch paper

How to measure. Record the dimensions on the sketch as you measure, in feet and inches as an architect would (you may also want to translate certain dimensions—such as those for tubs and shower enclosures—to inches). Measure to the nearest ⅛ inch, since even a fraction of an inch counts in fitting and spacing bathroom elements. All measurements should be taken to the wall, not to projecting wood trim or baseboards.

First, measure the room's dimensions—the floor, ceiling, and walls; measure each wall at counter height. To find out if the bathroom is square, measure the diagonals (corner to opposite corner). Don't fret if the room isn't square; just be sure your drawing reflects any irregularities.

With the overall dimensions recorded on your sketch, measure the fixtures and other elements of the room and the distances between them, and add this information to your sketch. You can use a wall-by-wall approach, or you can measure by category: fixtures, doors (and doorswings), windows, cabinetry, shelves, and accessories.

Depending on the extent of your remodeling goals, your sketch could include locations of the following: load-bearing walls and partitions, electrical outlets and switches, lights, drains, pipes, and vents. If you want to enlarge your bathroom—or just add more storage space—show relevant adjacent hall space, closets, rooms, and outdoor areas that you might be able to incorporate.

Note any heights that may affect your remodeling plans. These might include the clearance space under a duct or sloping ceiling, the floor-to-ceiling height, the floor-to-floor height in a two-story house, and the distance from the floor to the tops and bottoms of the windows.

Drawing to scale

The secrets to drawing a useful floor plan and elevations are a well-prepared sketch with accurate mea-

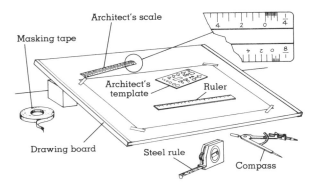

surements and a reasonable amount of skill at converting those measurements to the scale you choose. Your drawings don't have to be works of art, but they should be precise, complete, and easy to read.

Though architects often use a ¼-inch scale (¼ inch equals 1 foot), using a ½-inch scale for your bathroom remodeling drawings is easier, especially when you want to include all the elements of the room and write their dimensions. But if you want to use an architect's template to draw fixtures, make sure the scale of your drawing matches the template scale. Templates are commonly available in ¼-inch scale, but you should be able to find ½-inch templates if you telephone a few likely sources.

How to draw floor plans. With masking tape, attach the corners of the graph paper to a smooth working

surface. Use a ruler to draw all horizontal and vertical lines; make right angles exact. Use a compass to indicate doorswings.

To complete the floor plan, refer to your sketch and the sample finished floor plan below. Indicating walls and partitions by dark, thick lines will make the floor plan easier to read.

How to draw elevations. Drawing elevations is a matter of drawing straight-on views of your bathroom walls. Sketch the elements on each wall, measure carefully, and record the figures as you did for the floor plan; then redraw your elevation sketches on graph paper.

You can use one sheet for each wall, or draw all elevations on the same paper. With your sketch handy for reference, first draw the wall areas to scale, then fill in the fixtures and other elements.

EXISTING FLOOR PLAN & ELEVATIONS

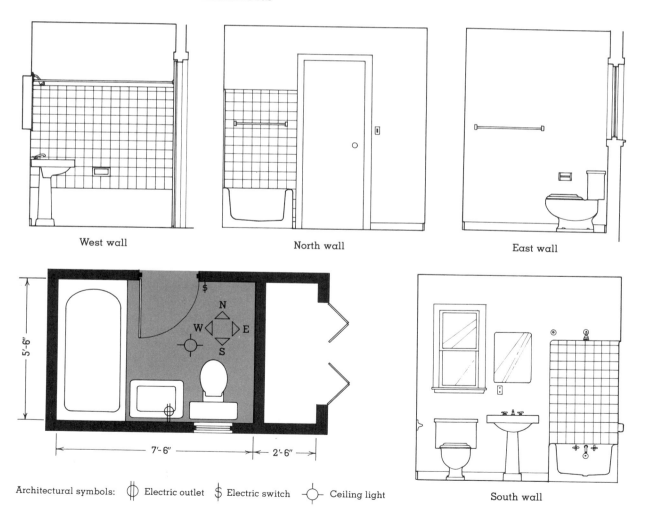

West wall

North wall

East wall

5'-6"

7'-6"   2'-6"

Architectural symbols: ⊕ Electric outlet $ Electric switch   ⊖ Ceiling light

South wall

The floor plan and elevations of your existing bathroom should look like the ones above. Be sure to add the appropriate architectural symbols to your floor plan to indicate electrical outlets and switches, windows, and lights.

Design: Basic considerations

By now you've analyzed your present bathroom's assets and liabilities. The next step is to look at the individual elements of design—line, shape, scale, color, texture, pattern, and light—and determine your style preferences. If you're planning plumbing, wiring, or structural alterations, or improvements to heating, cooling, or ventilating systems, you should incorporate them into your design.

Use the design information presented here to improve the efficiency and appearance of your bathroom; consider safety, too. Begin with a review of your remodeling goals. If you need to develop a new layout of fixtures, do it first and then incorporate storage, countertops, and various design elements.

Design is a creative process; take your time and enjoy it. Allow yourself to work without restrictions now; you can consider the limitations later. Let the ideas flow, and build on the ones you like.

What follows is a brief introduction to design concepts. You may want to do some research on certain subjects, or consult a designer or architect.

Determine your style

A room's style is like a melody, conveying structure, balance, harmony, and beauty. In bathrooms, style is determined by many factors—from architectural features to fixtures and accessories. To complement an existing bathroom or compose a new one, consider two things: the overall appearance of the room and its individual elements.

Where to look for ideas. We can't think of a better way for you to start collecting ideas than by studying the color photographs in this book. You'll find them on pages 1–16 and 49–80. Let these photos spur your imagination—you're almost certain to find ideas that you'd like to adapt to your own setting. Turn, too, to the "Bathroom showcase" on pages 31–40, where varied styles in fixtures and fittings are illustrated and described.

To collect more ideas and get a close look at new products, visit showrooms and stores displaying bathroom fixtures, cabinetry, light fixtures, wall coverings, tile, and flooring products. You can obtain catalogues, brochures, and color charts from these stores or from manufacturers. Seek out helpful salespersons and ask questions about products that interest you. Their answers and advice can be invaluable.

Start a notebook. As you accumulate notes, clippings, photographs, and brochures, file your remodeling ideas in a notebook. Choose a binder with several divisions (or file your material in separate 9 by 12-inch envelopes). Organize by subjects, such as best overall style, layouts and plans, pleasing color combinations, fixtures, lighting, and accessory ideas. Adapt the categories to suit your remodeling goals.

As your notebook fills with ideas, you'll quickly become aware of decorating trends that appeal to you. Perhaps you prefer a clean look with bold lines and bright colors, or a sculptured appearance enhanced with curves and restful pastels. Do you want a secluded bathroom with compartments or an open one with windows overlooking the garden?

You may also see some conflicts. A tile pattern may look impressive on the floor of a corridor-shaped bathroom, but lose its dramatic appeal in a bathroom with other dimensions. Try to identify what you like about certain styles, and work to combine elements of various designs.

Plumbing, wiring & structural changes

If the remodeling project you envision requires plumbing, wiring, or structural changes, consider these as you design your new bathroom. You may want to study the how-to section beginning on page 80 to familiarize yourself with the work that plumbing, wiring, and structural changes will entail. Some alterations are simple and inexpensive; others are more complicated and costly.

Generally, you can move your sink a few inches with only minor plumbing changes. Your existing supply and drain lines can usually support a second sink. You can extend existing supply and drain lines if the distance from the vent is less than the maximum distance allowed by your local code. If not, you'll have to install a secondary vent—a major undertaking.

If your bathroom has a wood floor with a crawlspace or basement underneath, it's relatively simple to move the plumbing and wiring. But, if the room has a concrete floor, you'll find it's an expensive proposition to move plumbing or wiring that's located under the concrete. To gain access to the plumbing and wiring, you'd have to go through the laborious process of breaking up and removing the concrete.

Repositioning electrical outlets and switches or adding electrical boxes for light fixtures involves opening walls or the ceiling. The cost of these changes depends on how easy it is to gain access to the wiring, and how far you move the switches, outlets, and fixtures from their present locations.

Structural changes, especially changes entailing work on load-bearing walls, fall into the category of serious remodeling. Relocating a door or window opening involves a lot of work, including framing and finishing, but adding a partition wall is an easier and less expensive job.

Heating & ventilation

Ventilation fans are relatively simple to add or relocate. These units are installed between joists in the ceiling or between studs in the wall, and may require duct work to the outside. Local building codes may specify the

PLAYING IT SAFE IN THE BATHROOM

About 25 percent of all home accidents occur in the bathroom. You can reduce the risk of injury by precautionary planning and by encouraging safe practices.

- Install sufficient lighting. Include a night light, especially if you have small children.
- Choose tempered glass, plastic, or other shatterproof materials for construction and accessories.
- Install locks that can be opened from the outside in an emergency.
- Locate clothes hooks above eye level.
- Select a tub or shower with a nonslip surface. For existing fixtures, use a rubber bath mat.
- Install L-shaped or horizontal grab rails, capable of supporting a person weighing 250 pounds, in tub and shower areas. Installation must be done properly—bracing between studs may be required.

Plaster-mounted accessories don't provide sufficient support.

- Anchor any carpeting. Choose area rugs or bathmats with nonskid backing.
- Avoid scalding by lowering the setting of your water heater (see page 41) or installing a mixing valve to mix hot and cold water to a preset point and to prevent sudden changes in temperature.
- Test the water temperature before stepping into a shower or tub and when assisting a child or elderly person.
- If children live in or visit your house, buy medicines (and, when possible, household cleansers) in childproof containers. Store these items in a cabinet with a safety latch. Tape seldom-used nonsafety containers closed.
- Never take medications in the dark. Check the contents of your medi-

cine cabinet at least twice a year, and discard outdated medicines and those with unreadable or incomplete directions.

- Be sure electrical outlets are grounded and protected with GFCI circuit breakers. Outlets should be out of reach from shower or bathtub. Install safety covers over unused outlets.
- Avoid using electric appliances in wet areas. Keep portable heaters out of the bathroom.
- Store electric appliances out of children's reach. Never leave small children unattended in the bathroom. Keep the door securely closed whenever the bathroom is not in use.
- Post phone numbers of the nearest emergency rescue unit and poison control center.
- Keep a first aid kit handy for use in an emergency.

---

placement of exhaust fans within the bathroom; check the codes before you complete your design.

If you want to extend your existing heating system to a bathroom, check with a professional to be sure your system can handle the added load without a loss of efficiency. You can relocate a hot air register in the floor or in the vanity kickspace by changing the duct work beneath the floor; ducts for wall registers can be rerouted in the stud wall. If you're adding a register, locate it where the duct work can be extended easily from the existing system and where you won't sacrifice wall space.

Hot-air duct work is best done by a heating or sheet metal contractor. Extending hot water or steam systems is easier, but it, too, calls for a professional to do the work. It may be more practical to equip your bathroom with an electric space heater (which can be recessed in the wall or ceiling) or an electric heat lamp.

Drawing your designs

One of the biggest challenges in designing your new bathroom is keeping track of your ideas. If they're really

flowing, you don't want to forget your best inspirations because you didn't get them on paper.

One solution is to use paper cutouts and then sketch your best ideas as they come to you. First, draw the perimeter of your existing floor plan and adjacent areas to be included in the project, such as closets or halls. Use graph paper to make cutouts (to scale) of fixtures, cabinets, countertops, and other elements—both existing features you plan to keep and new ones to be added.

Move the cutouts around within the perimeter of the floor plan, and when you hit on a layout you like, sketch it so you won't forget it. When you've accumulated several sketches, compare and evaluate them.

You can use the cutout technique with the elevation sketches of your present bathroom. You'll prepare a different set of cutouts—straight-on views of fixtures, cabinets, mirrors, and other elements on or against the room's walls. Arrange these cutouts with an eye for line, shape, and scale. They'll help you visualize the room as a whole and see relationships between horizontal, vertical, diagonal, and curved lines. Sketch the arrangements you like so you can compare them.

Design: Layout & sample floor plans

One of the most important elements of design is layout. In the bathroom, this refers primarily to the shape and size of the room and the arrangement of fixtures, as well as the space needed to use each unit, the amount of counter and storage space needed, and the locations of doors, windows, and partitions.

The "best" bathroom layout doesn't exist—good layouts vary dramatically. Generally, though, a workable layout provides for good access to the room, easy movement within the room, and the convenient use of fixtures and storage units.

Whether you need to relocate one or all of your fixtures, you'll want a layout that works smoothly for all members of your household. After you read the following information, study the sample floor plans carefully. Then experiment with your own bathroom layout, using the technique described on page 23.

Minimum clearances

Community building codes specify minimum required clearances between, beside, and in front of bathroom fixtures to allow adequate room for use, cleaning, and repair. Your bathroom's layout must meet the minimum standards. If you have more room than required, you can enjoy added flexibility.

Generally, you can locate side-by-side fixtures closer together than fixtures positioned opposite each other. If a sink is opposite a bathtub or toilet, 30 inches is the minimum distance between them. Children and elderly and handicapped persons may require assistance or special fixtures; if you anticipate such needs, allow extra space in your layout.

The illustration below shows some standard heights and minimum clearances to help you in initial planning; use them as a guide to arranging fixtures and room layout.

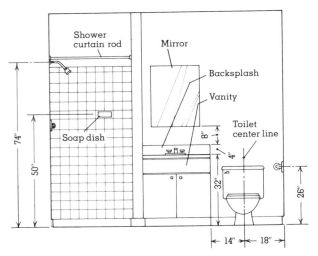

Elevation drawing indicates standard heights, minimum clearances, and recommendations for the positioning of accessories.

Common bathroom layouts

The four most common layouts are classified by the arrangement of fixtures.

• **The one-wall bathroom.** This layout suits a long, narrow room—as narrow as 4½ feet. It's an economical layout because all the plumbing—connections, drains, and vents—is in one wall.

• **The L-shaped bathroom.** In this layout, fixtures are arranged in an L; a bathtub usually occupies the short leg. Commonly used for 5 by 7-foot or 5 by 8-foot bathrooms, this design provides ample floor space. All the plumbing is in one wall.

• **The corridor bathroom.** Access is a feature of this layout, with fixtures located along two opposite walls. It's a practical arrangement for a small bathroom tucked between two bedrooms, with a door to each. The corridor should be at least 30 inches wide. Two walls require plumbing.

• **The U-shaped bathroom.** In a square room, fixtures are often placed along three walls. Though practical to use, the U-shaped layout requires plumbing in all three walls.

Arranging fixtures & storage

Before you experiment with layouts, note the dimensions of the room, of adjacent space to be included, and of existing fixtures or their replacements. The more facts you have available, the easier it will be to work with your layouts. You'll keep costs down and simplify remodeling if you select a layout that uses the existing water supply and drain lines and vent stack.

To begin, position the largest unit—the bathtub or shower—allowing space for convenient access, for cleaning, and (if needed) for bathing a child.

Next, place the sink (or sinks). The most frequently used fixture in the bathroom, it should be positioned out of the traffic zone. Be sure to plan for ample room in front for reaching below the sink, and plenty of elbow room at the sides.

Locate the toilet (and bidet, if you have one) away from the door; often the toilet is positioned beside the tub or shower. If space permits, you can improve privacy with a partition or compartment. A toilet and bidet should be placed alongside each other.

After arranging the fixtures, plan your storage space. Consider what you need to store, how much space you need, and how to organize it. If you need to increase your storage capacity, review your notes from the inventory to pinpoint which items require space. Consider equipping a vanity or cabinet with racks, shelves, pull-outs, and lazy susans for supplies. Many bathroom items are candidates for open storage—why not display colorful towels and stacks of soap on open shelving? For a look at a variety of successful storage solutions, see pages 76–79.

SAMPLE FLOOR PLANS

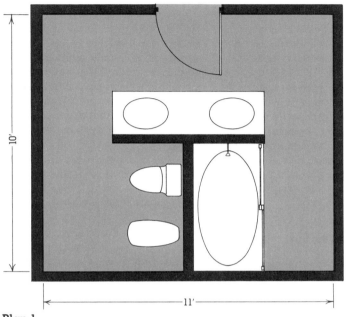

Plan 1

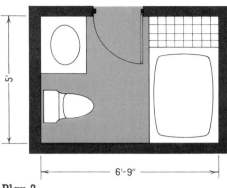

Plan 2

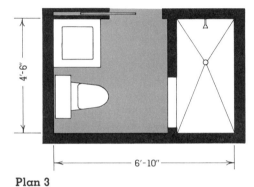

Plan 3

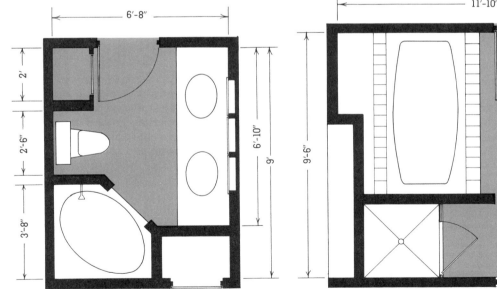

Plan 4

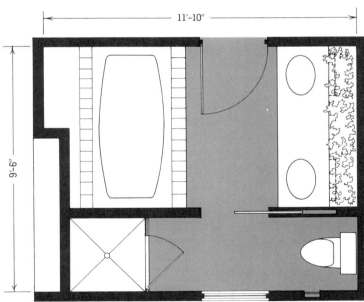

Plan 5

1. Clustering of fixtures offers easy access to sinks in an almost-square bathroom. You can use the tub/shower, toilet, and bidet in semiprivacy; for more seclusion, add sliding or bifold doors. **2.** Corridor layout suits this standard-size bathroom. The sink and toilet have plenty of clearance along the 5-foot wall. A soaking tub, set in a platform, substitutes for a standard-size recessed tub. **3.** A room with a shower, toilet, and sink is often called a three-quarter bathroom. The sliding door provides convenient access and avoids the doorswing

dilemma. **4.** Compartments, counter space, and a corner tub/shower characterize this spacious children's bathroom. The layout provides generous floor space and ample storage. **5.** This master bathroom suite contains an oversize whirlpool tub—large enough for two people—in a raised and tiled platform, and a separate shower. The chambers are separated by a sliding door; each chamber has a window. Medicine cabinets are built into a window planter located behind the sinks. Design for 4 and 5: Moyer Associates Architects.

MORE THAN JUST BATHS

Today we take bathrooms for granted, but it wasn't until the Victorian era that bathrooms were planned as a separate room inside the house. Even the White House waited until 1850 to get its own bathtub.

In recent decades, the bathroom has really come into its own. Stylish fixtures and fittings, easy-care materials, and accessories in an unlimited palette of vibrant colors have encouraged imaginative design and decorating ideas.

No longer merely a utilitarian space, today's bathroom reflects the personality and interests of its owners. More than just a room for bathing and grooming, it can be a cheerful refuge or a serene place for solitude.

It's a place where you can indulge a fantasy or two by choosing an oversize or tiled tub or shower; or perhaps you'd prefer a sunken tub or Japanese soaking tub—or even a circular or oval model. In cold climates, a small fireplace would quell the chill on winter nights.

To add character and make the room uniquely yours, consider special touches—a private deck or garden, space for reading material or for displaying art, a handsome claw-foot tub, an exercise area. For inspiration, browse through our gallery of ideas for transforming the bathroom into your own private retreat.

Keeping fit at home

Everything a body needs to keep in shape can be assembled in a home fitness center.

Your choice of equipment will be governed by the space available to you and by your personal health regime. Perhaps you enjoy pedaling a stationary cycle or building strength with a rowing machine or barbells. If you prefer flexibility or ballet *barre* exercises, you may want to feature a mirrored wall, an exercise bar (mounted with strong handrail brackets), and ample space for floor exercises. If you're counting calories, a doctor's scale will help you measure your progress.

Sun lovers may want to build in a tanning platform and equipment to maintain a suntan through gloomy days. Sometimes a sauna or whirlpool-spa unit is part of a master suite.

If space for exercising is limited, you might build a wall-mounted *ribbstol* (pronounced rib-stool); developed in Sweden, this sturdy ladderlike unit (illustrated below) can be used for sit-ups, leg lifts, elevated push-ups, and ballet exercises. It's built of fir 2 by 6s and fourteen 3-foot lengths of pine dowels; most rungs are spaced 5 inches apart. The unit is lag-bolted securely to the wall studs.

Everything within easy reach

You'll save dressing time and energy when you house your clothing in an efficiently arranged wall or walk-in closet adjacent to the bathroom. To avoid moisture damage, be sure the bath is well ventilated. You can close off the closet with sliding or bifold doors.

To unify the dressing area with the nearby bedroom and bath, extend or coordinate wall covering and flooring materials. Mirrored walls or doors help create an illusion of more space and greater depth.

Put your best face forward

If you have an otherwise wasted corner, turn it into a makeup center where all the necessities for good grooming are kept in one place. Your

Doubling as a home fitness center, this bathroom features a stationary cycle and a ladderlike *ribbstol* for exercising.

dressing table can be a purchased, self-contained unit or a counter with built-in storage.

You'll want a large single or triple-paneled mirror, well lighted for close-up viewing. Theatrical bulbs rimming the mirror can add a dramatic touch. Incandescent lighting is usually kinder to skin tones than most kinds of fluorescent lighting; for information on lighting and fixtures, see pages 30 and 38.

Store your grooming paraphernalia in compartmentalized trays or drawers; be sure you have an electrical outlet handy for using small appliances.

Art in the bathroom

Why not showcase handicrafts or a favorite piece of art as part of your bathroom decor?

If you want to incorporate crafts into your design, work with a craftsperson to achieve the desired effect. You might include a pattern of hand-painted ceramic tiles in the shower or around the rim of the sink or tub. Or you could feature a colorful stained glass panel, backlighted by sun or artificial light to highlight its striking design. You can also display favorite pieces of folk art or crafts.

You may want to hang a favorite print. Such art should be framed and sealed against moisture; tell your framer if you plan to hang a piece of art in a moist environment.

A nook for reading

If you enjoy reading in uninterrupted solitude, why not incorporate a small library for private browsing in your bathroom? It can be as simple as a shelf to hold a colorful collection of paperbacks, or a rack to display the latest magazines. A skylighted alcove

Linger awhile in this luxurious bathroom to enjoy the oversize tub, a display of arts and crafts, a private garden, and a nook for leisurely reading.

with a pillowed bench offers a particularly delightful place for leisurely reading and daydreaming.

Bring the outdoors in

Can you take advantage of a view of trees, mountains, or water? If so, feature it in your remodeling and enjoy a vista of the world outside.

In a private garden off the bath, you can enjoy leafy greenery and containers of bright blooms that you change with the seasons. Often gardens are viewed through a window wall bordering the tub or shower; access is usually through a sliding glass door in the bathroom or from an adjacent bedroom or hallway. If you want

to linger in the sun, add a small deck or patio. Privacy walls shield you from the outside world.

Another way to enjoy the view is to install a window over the bathroom sink—perhaps one of the greenhouse windows available from building supply stores and home improvement centers. Or build a planter inside or outside the window, where you can grow your favorite plants.

A few judiciously placed house plants add a splash of style to the bathroom. Be sure to choose varieties that thrive in moisture and humidity, and shield them from direct sun. Hanging plants suspended from ceiling beams or hooks are perfect for the bathroom.

Design: Line, shape & scale

A room bombards your senses with myriad impressions—some that you like, others that you dislike—and the signals come through loud and clear, even though you might find it difficult to put into words the reasons for those vivid reactions.

Three keys to understanding design are line, shape, and scale. Take another look at your bathroom elevation sketches to examine these elements. You may want to improve the existing conditions—or perhaps you'll decide to try an entirely new approach.

Line—the dominant theme

Designs incorporate different kinds of lines—vertical, horizontal, diagonal, angular, and curved. One line usually dominates, characterizing the design of a room. Vertical lines give a sense of height; horizontal lines add width; and diagonals suggest movement. Depending on their use, curved and angular lines impart a sense of grace and dynamism.

If you repeat similar lines, you give a room a sense of unity. Look at your elevation sketches: do you see an orderly or a jumbled pattern in the arrangement of vertical lines created by the shower or tub unit, cabinets, countertops, windows, doors, and mirrors? Does the horizontal line marking the top of the window match those created by the tops of the shower stall, door, and mirror? If you plan to add or rearrange elements that affect the vertical and horizontal line-up, be sure to consider alignment in your new design. For an example of how all this works, compare the drawing here with the elevation drawing for the south wall on page 21. Clearly, not everything can or should align, but the effect is far more pleasing if a number of elements do align—particularly the highest features in the room.

Depending on the shape and size of your bathroom, you may want to emphasize or subdue certain lines to create a particular effect. For example, you can make a narrower room appear wider and more spacious by add-ing horizontal lines—rows of open shelves, tiles on the sink backsplash, or long towel bars.

Shape—a sense of harmony

Continuity and compatibility in shape also contribute to a unified design. Of course, you needn't repeat the same shape throughout the room—carried too far, that becomes a monotonous proposition.

Study the shapes created by doorways, windows, counters, fixtures, and other elements. Look at patterns in your flooring, wall covering, shower curtain, and towels. Are they different or similar? If they're different, do they clash? If they're similar, are they boring? Consider ways to complement existing shapes or add compatible new ones—for example, you could repeat the arch over a recessed bathtub in the shape of a doorway or in shelf trim.

Scale—everything in proportion

When the scale of bathroom elements is in proportion to the overall size of the room, the design usually appears harmonious. A small bathroom seems even smaller if equipped with large fixtures and a large vanity. But the same bathroom appears larger, or at least in scale, when equipped with space-saving fixtures, a petite vanity, and open shelves.

Consider the proportions of adjacent features as well. When wall cabinets or linen shelves extend to the ceiling, they often make a room seem top-heavy—and therefore smaller. To counteract this look without losing storage space, you can divide the cabinet doors into sections, with smaller units at the top. Reposition shelving so top shelves are relatively close together and shelves at the bottom—serving as anchors—are farther apart. Let your floor plan and elevation drawings provide clues to ways you can modify the scale of different elements, improving your bathroom design.

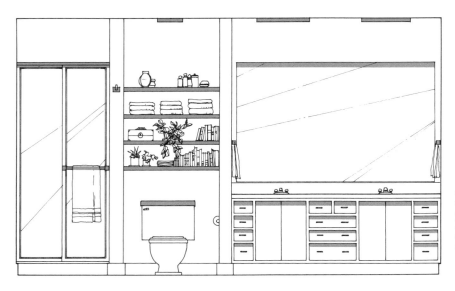

Alignment of horizontal planes (in blue) shows how line creates a harmonious design. Notice the relationships among lines along the wall and within each compartment. For example, the toilet tank top and vanity door tops are at the same height; the first shelf and the towel bar on the shower door are in alignment.

Design: Color, texture & pattern

The ways you use color, texture, and pattern play an important part in your design. Of these, color is unquestionably the dominant factor—it affects the way a person perceives space; it interacts with lighting; it triggers emotions. Properly applied, color can accentuate or camouflage architectural features.

In selecting colors, textures, and patterns for your bathroom, remember that you will live with your choices for a long time. Brilliant red or electric blue may appeal to you at the moment, but would you like being greeted by such intense color every morning for the next several years? Bright yellow can give a bathroom a cheerful look on gray winter days, but it may be overpowering in summer.

Before you buy any fixtures or materials, use colored pencils or felt-tip markers to experiment with different combinations on copies of your floor plan and elevation drawings. You'll consider such questions as where you want to place color accents and whether a large or small tile pattern is best for your bathroom.

After you narrow down your selections, make a sample board to see how your choices work together. Color charts for fixtures are readily available, as are sample paint chips, fabric swatches, wallpaper samples, and flooring materials.

Choosing your colors

Personal preferences will play the leading role as you develop your color scheme. You'll also want to consider how lighting affects color, the mood you want to create, and the size and orientation of your bathroom.

Learn the guidelines. Color has three dimensions: hue, value, and intensity.

- **Hue** is the attribute that determines a color's position in the spectrum.

- **Value** refers to a color's lightness or darkness, determined by the amount of white or black in it.

- **Intensity** refers to a color's brightness or dullness; a pure color has the most intensity.

Many variables affect color: surface, texture, lighting, and surrounding colors. For example, a color appears glossy on a hard, smooth surface, yet on a more absorbent surface, the same color looks duller.

To make a small room appear larger, use light colors that have a light value and bright intensity. Light colors reflect the light and make surfaces appear larger and farther apart. Dark colors absorb light, making surfaces appear smaller and closer together. Too much color contrast has a similar effect and reduces the sense of space.

Be cautious about covering surfaces with bright, intense colors. It's usually best to use these colors for accessories, which are relatively inexpensive to replace if you grow tired of the color.

In any environment, colors affect each other. A color's hue, value, and intensity can all change when another color is introduced into a room.

Since the same color appears different under various types of light, it's best to select your colors under the kind of light—natural, incandescent, fluorescent—that you'll have in your bathroom.

Depending on the direction your bathroom faces, you may want to use warm or cool colors to enhance or counteract the natural light.

Orange, yellow, and red convey warmth and make spaces seem compact; blues and greens make a room appear cool and spacious.

Select a color scheme. Among the most popular combinations are those that employ complementary or monochromatic colors.

Complementary color schemes, which use contrasting hues, pair warm colors (yellow, orange, red) with cool ones (violet, blue, and green). Pairing contrasting colors gives a vibrant, exciting look; often both appear more attractive. To prevent a clash, use hues of different values—a lighter tint or darker shade of one—and different intensity. This variation also works effectively when you use colors adjacent in the spectrum, such as blue and green or yellow and orange.

Contrasting colors also work well as accents, drawing attention to interesting features or structural elements. But if you want to conceal a problem, it's best to use a single color in the trouble area.

Monochromatic color schemes combine several colors in the same family, such as navy blue, sky blue, and pale blue; for best results, one color should be dominant. Monochromatic schemes convey a mood of restfulness and serenity.

Adding interest with texture & pattern

You can bring imaginative ideas to a bathroom through careful selection of textures and patterns. Materials commonly used in bathrooms range from rough wood to glossy tile. Rough textures absorb light, subdue colors, and convey informality. Smooth surfaces reflect light and suggest a more formal, modern wood.

When you're selecting flooring and wall covering materials, you'll find a seemingly endless array of patterns. First consider the size of your bathroom. If it's small, choose wall and floor coverings carefully. Some patterns, such as those with large or complex designs, can make a small room appear smaller. If you're unsure how a pattern will affect the room, consult a professional or choose an unobstrusive pattern in a light color.

Though variation in texture and pattern adds interest, too much variety has a disastrous effect. Choose one strong feature or dominant pattern as your focus, then select other surfaces to complement it. Intricate tile work or wallpaper with a tropical print, for example, may be all the pattern you need in a bathroom.

Design: Light

No matter how beautifully it is decorated, a bathroom with inadequate lighting will be an unpleasant place to be—and difficult to use. Comfortable light levels are a matter of individual preference. Some people are accustomed to brightly lighted rooms; other people feel more relaxed and secure in relatively low light levels.

For many years Americans have lived in relative brightness indoors. But with the new accent on energy conservation, the current trend is toward providing bright lighting in task areas, with surroundings more softly lit.

In a multiple-use room such as a bathroom, the light levels required range from very soft ambient light to strong directional task lighting. Usually you can achieve a pleasing level by bringing in natural light through windows and skylights, and supplementing it with artificial lighting.

Natural light

To bring natural light into your bathroom, you can use windows and doors (opening to secluded areas) as well as skylights—alone or in combination.

A single window in the middle of a wall often creates a glaring contrast with the surrounding area. To increase the amount of natural light, consider placing windows on adjacent walls or installing a skylight—either will provide more uniform lighting over a larger area. To avoid unwanted heat and glare, it's best to locate windows and skylights so they have a north or east exposure.

Depending on your climate and the orientation of your bathroom, you may need to consider ways to control unwanted heat loss or gain—for example, extending the roof overhang or installing blinds, translucent shades or curtains, or tinted glass.

Artificial lighting

Since only one or two bathroom activities will be going on simultaneously, you probably won't need to have all the room's lights on at once. Consider a variety of light levels, sources, and controls to meet various needs.

Task lighting. To begin, look at the work or activity areas in your bathroom where the more exacting visual tasks—such as shaving, applying makeup, and reading—take place. Pinpoint areas where you want to locate task lighting, such as sink, mirror, counter, toilet, and storage units, and consider how precise and demanding the tasks are.

Light bulbs & tubes

Light bulbs and tubes can be grouped in general categories according to the way they produce light. For household lighting, the choices are between incandescent and fluorescent, both of which can be used for task

and general lighting. Generally, a combination gives the most pleasing results.

When you select bulbs and tubes, consider their wattage, level of output, energy efficiency, shape, size, cost, life, and compatability with fixtures. You'll also want to think about the amounts and kinds of color that different bulbs and tubes emit.

How much light do you need in the bathroom? If you use incandescent bulbs, plan to provide 3½ to 4 watts per square foot; with fluorescent bulbs and tubes, provide 1½ to 2 watts per square foot. Recommended wattages per square foot for incandescent and fluorescent lighting may be lower in communities that have adopted residential energy standards. Check your building code for regulations that may apply where you live.

If you're concerned about energy efficiency, you may also want to include dimmers and timers in your lighting plan. By reducing the electrical current consumed, solid-state dimmers save energy and extend the life of bulbs, because filaments burn at lower temperatures.

Incandescent light. The standard in homes, this kind of light is produced by a fine tungsten wire that burns slowly inside a glass bulb. Though it provides a warm and flattering ambience, it also generates a lot of heat, which may not be desirable.

Daylight or sunlight appears white, but actually contains the full spectrum of colors; incandescent light includes colors from most of the spectrum, but has a larger proportion of yellow and red than sunlight does. When dimmed, it becomes more orange and red.

Fluorescent light. This light is produced when electrical energy and mercury vapor create an arc that stimulates the phosphors coating the inside of the tube. Because the light comes evenly from the whole surface of the tube, it spreads in all directions, creating a steady, shadowless light. Compared to incandescent bulbs, fluorescent tubes are three times as energy efficient, last longer, operate at a lower temperature, and are cheaper to use.

Fluorescent tubes require a ballast to light the tubes and maintain the electrical flow. Ballasts for 4-foot tubes are usually quieter than those for other sizes. Check that the tubes and ballasts are the rapid or instant-start variety that light without flickering or delay. If you want to lower energy costs, use energy-saver tubes.

Fluorescent light is generally thought to be low in red and high in green and blue light waves, but in fact there are more than 200 "colors" of fluorescent tubes available. Some of the new fluorescent tubes are called "full spectrum" and come extremely close to daylight in color. If you plan to mix incandescent and fluorescent lighting, deluxe warm white (soft white) is probably the best fluorescent choice.

Bathroom showcase

Our "bathroom showcase" is a wonderland of products and materials. Here you can see and compare a sampling of styles, installation methods, functions, and materials at a glance. The showcase can tell you which sink is the easiest to install, which tub is the heaviest, which toilet the quietest. Information about ceramic tile and other materials commonly used in the bathroom and in the manufacture of fixtures is on pages 39–40.

Though by no means exhaustive, the showcase provides basic facts to help you plan your project, from drawing new bathroom layouts, to preparing specifications for contracts or ordering, to developing a budget. Use this section to prepare for the shopping experience—an exciting but time-consuming part of remodeling.

One advantage professional remodelers have over do-it-yourselfers is a broad, up-to-date knowledge of products and materials. These pages offer you an opportunity to acquire some of that knowledge. You don't have to become an expert, but you should know that most products and materials differ in quality, style, size, shape, color, efficiency, and cost. Even though you may be trying to economize on your remodeling, when you shop, let quality be your guide.

Shopping for quality

Bathroom products—fixtures, fittings, tile, vanities, light fixtures—are usually priced according to quality. More expensive products usually last longer, look better, and function more efficiently. In the case of faucets and other fittings, though, a higher price often reflects the expense of the finish, not the quality of the fitting itself. Economy items from reputable firms are likely to be well made, but they're often less attractive than their costlier cousins.

When you shop, consider function, durability, and esthetic appeal as well as price. Ceramic tile, for example, is more expensive than some other wall coverings, but it requires minimum maintenance and can last a lifetime. Vanities with basins are more expensive than wall-hung basins, but vanities provide more storage space. You may like the efficiency of a one-piece toilet, but the nostalgic look of a pull-chain toilet may appeal to you more.

If you're stretching a budget, it's wise to purchase fixtures and fittings of the best quality you can afford. They are permanent and cost no more to install than lower-quality ones. You can always upgrade floor, wall, and countertop surfaces or other items later. If you can find the products and materials you want on sale, take advantage of the savings. But before you buy, inspect sale merchandise carefully for damage and finish defects, and find out whether a warranty applies. Ask a salesperson if you're in doubt about why an item is being offered at a reduced price. Sometimes lower prices reflect insignificant or undetectable flaws, such as color variations.

What materials are best?

Smooth, nonabsorbent, and easy-to-clean materials are most often recommended for bathrooms. In some communities, materials are specified by code. Your building inspector can tell you which materials, if any, are off limits.

Glass, marble, glazed ceramic tile, plastic laminate, fiberglass-reinforced plastic, vitreous china, and porcelain enameled steel and cast iron are good choices for the bathroom because they're just about impervious to water. Surfaces with particularly lustrous finishes, such as glazed ceramic tile, are less likely to show water spots and splashes than glass and plastic laminate are. Wood can pose a problem: untreated, it will discolor, warp, stain, and decay if exposed to water. If you use wood, thoroughly protect it on all sides with a good sealer such as polyurethane. Pay particular attention when sealing the joints, so that moisture won't cause hidden damage underneath the wood.

In choosing materials, consider the ease or difficulty of installation and how the required installation method may affect maintenance and appearance. If you install floor tile, for example, you'll have to contend with seams or joints. Depending on the size of your floor, you may want to install sheet flooring instead. Sheet flooring is available in widths up to 12 feet; the 6-foot width is convenient to install in many standard-size bathrooms. You'll find more information about bathroom materials on page 40.

Consider conservation

Water and energy conservation are high priorities for many bathroom remodelers. If you plan to replace fixtures and fittings, look at those specifically designed to save water and energy.

Many manufacturers offer water-saving toilets, faucets, shower heads, and hand-held shower attachments at prices comparable to those of their conventional counterparts. They require no special installation, and they operate with no loss of efficiency because their water-saving capabilities are part of their design. These fixtures and fittings can reduce the amount of water used and the amount of energy needed to heat water for bathing and cleaning.

Water-saver toilets, discussed on page 37, use only about 3 gallons of water per flush, compared to 5 to 7 gallons used by conventional toilets. Many of the fittings on page 36 are available in water-saving models. Some fittings have flow-control devices that reduce the flow while maintaining the spray force. Others have aerators or fine mesh screens that break the water into droplets. Before you purchase any fixtures or fittings, review the merits of different brands and choose the ones that are best for you. To save energy when lighting your bathroom, see page 30. For conservation tips on heating water, see page 41.

SINKS

Sinks are available in many shapes, sizes, colors, materials, and styles. The most commonly available styles are wall-hung, deck-mount, integral bowl, and pedestal. Sink backs can be flat, slanted, or designed with a ledge. Sinks either have no holes for fittings or they have holes for 4, 6, or 8-inch faucet assemblies; some also have holes for spray attachments and lotion dispensers (see page 36 for information about sink fittings). Standard heights from the floor to the sink rim are 31 to 36 inches. Common materials are vitreous china, synthetic marble, fiberglass-reinforced plastic, acrylic, enameled cast iron, and enameled steel.

Styles	Characteristics
Wall-hung  	Wall-hung sinks come with hangers or angle brackets for support. If you replace one wall-hung sink with another, change the bracket as well. If you're installing a wall-hung sink for the first time, plan to tear out part of the wall. These sinks are the least expensive, easiest to install, and most compact.
Deck-mount, self-rimming  	A self-rimming sink has a molded overlap that's supported by the edge of the countertop cutout. The mounting hole in the countertop is undersized, allowing the sink rim to sit on the countertop. This style is easy to install and offers the widest range in shapes, including shell, hexagon, and fluted.
Deck-mount, flush  	A surrounding metal frame holds a flush-mount sink to the countertop. The frames are available in several finishes to match fittings. Keeping the joints between the frame, sink, and countertop clean requires some vigilance. This style is usually used with plastic laminate countertops.
Deck-mount, unrimmed  	An unrimmed sink is recessed beneath the countertop opening and held in place by metal clips. Fittings are mounted through the countertop or on the sink. The sink-countertop joint requires a little extra effort to keep clean. This sink is a good choice for use with countertops of synthetic marble, tile, or plastic laminate.
Integral bowl & countertop  	Made of synthetic marble, vitreous china, or fiberglass, an integral bowl and countertop has no joints, so installation and cleaning are easy. This one-piece molded unit sits on top of a vanity or cabinet. Predrilled holes for fittings are part of the package. Double-bowl units are available.
Pedestal  	Pedestal sinks have made a comeback, thanks to their clean, contemporary look. Made of vitreous china, these elegant towers hide the pipes. Some models have splayed pedestals so pipes are visible from the side. Pedestal basins are easy to install and to clean around. They're among the highest priced basins. But if you're accustomed to storage space under the basin, you'll have to rethink your storage situation.

VANITIES

A vanity is a welcome sight in a room full of fixtures and fittings. In many bathrooms, it's the only piece of furniture and offers the only surface for displaying decorative accessories. You'll appreciate this cousin to the cabinet for many reasons.

Vanities hide sink plumbing and can provide counter space. Depending on their design, they offer cabinets, shelves, drawers, and towel bars to storage-shy bathrooms.

Vanities also impart style. Like furniture and other kinds of cabinetry, vanities are made in contemporary, colonial, provincial, and traditional styles. These styles are usually characterized by the type and placement of trim on vanity drawers and doors. The fixtures used with vanity sinks accent the style.

When you shop for a vanity, you can purchase the base with or without countertop and deck-mount sink; you also can buy integral countertops and sinks for vanities. Some manufacturers also produce modular cabinet and shelf units for use with their vanities; other modular units for use with vanities include laundry bins, medicine cabinets, and closets. If it's not practical to purchase all you want at once, you can add units later. The key is planning—make sure you leave room for additions and plan your sink installation accordingly.

Vanities are made in many sizes. A standard width is 30 inches, increasing at 3 or 6-inch intervals. Vanities are as narrow as 12 inches and as wide as 60 inches. Standard heights vary from 28 to 36 inches, and depths from 18 to 21 inches.

Whether you select sleek plastic or warm wood, quality construction and materials should be your first consideration. Vanity bases are made of wood, particle board, or both, and feature a variety of constuction techniques. Look for solid and secure joints; the best are glued. Doors and drawers should open and close smoothly and easily. Check on other details such as interior finish, adjustable shelves, and sturdy hinges and pulls. Bases may be surfaced with wood veneers, plastic veneers, or plastic laminate. Solid wood and wood veneers may be oiled, stained, or painted; you can also carve and then finish solid wood doors.

Molded integral sinks for vanities are usually made of synthetic marble, fiberglass, or vitreous china. Because these units have no joints, they're easy to clean.

Plastic laminate, ceramic tile, synthetic marble, and marble are used to surface vanity countertops. Some of these materials are attached to a subsurface, usually exterior plywood. Wood is sometimes used for countertops, too. To prevent water damage, the surface of wood countertops should be finished with a sealant. Countertops have either square edges and corners or rounded edges and corners. Your choice may be limited or affected by the material or method of manufacture.

Styles

Pedestal   Molded top   Wall-hung   Washstand

Modular   Extended counter   Double-bowl

SHOWERS

If you have oversize doors in your house, you may be able to use a one-piece molded shower or tub/shower surround in your bathroom remodeling, but these units are used primarily in new houses or additions.

Many options are available to remodelers, including shower and tub/shower kits that come with or without overlapping wall panels, adhesive, and caulking. You can also purchase shower and tub/shower wall kits to use with existing shower bases and tubs. If shower or tub/shower doors don't come with your kit, you can buy them separately. Size is important; make sure you carefully measure the installation area and the unit before you buy. Units are available in fiberglass-reinforced plastic, acrylic, plastic laminate, and synthetic marble. Shower stalls made of tin or stainless steel are fading from the plumbing scene.

Styles	Characteristics
Shower surrounds 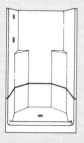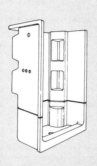	Shower surrounds require framing for support; you fasten the panel flanges to the framing. The shower base, walls, and door can be purchased individually or in a kit. Some models come with ceilings. For comfort, choose a shower that's at least 3 feet square. Complete assemblies vary in height, but 84 inches is common. Corner and circular shower models are available. Circular showers feature clear or tinted acrylic doors that double as walls.
Tub/shower surrounds 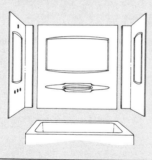	Tub/shower surrounds also must have framing for support. You can purchase the tub, walls, and door in a kit, or buy a separate recessed tub and match it with compatible prefabricated wall panels or a custom wall treatment (such as tile panels). Molded fiberglass wall panels may include molded soap dishes, ledges, and grab bars. You can also add a shower head or install a hand-held shower attachment to convert an existing tub surround to a tub/shower. Shower attachments are mounted to the wall, tub spout, or shower head.
Shower bases Rectangular Square Corner	A shower base can be purchased separately or in a kit that includes a shower surround. Most bases are made of fiberglass, acrylic, or terrazzo, and come in standard sizes in rectangular, square, and corner models with a predrilled hole for the drain.
Shower doors 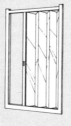 Swinging Sliding Folding	Doors for showers come in a variety of styles: swinging, sliding, and folding, as well as pivot (not shown). For tub/showers, the choice includes sliding and folding doors. Door manufacturers may also make matching shower and tub/shower surrounds. Doors and enclosures are commonly made of tempered safety glass with aluminum frames. Frames come in many finishes; you can select one to match your fittings. The glazing can be clear, hammered, pebbled, tinted, or striped. Many sliding doors have towel bars. Swinging, folding, and pivot doors can be installed with right or left openings. Folding doors are constructed of rigid plastic panels or flexible plastic sheeting.

BATHTUBS

Today's bathtub market overflows with styles. The 30 by 60-inch bathtub, which contributed to the predominance of the 5 by 7-foot bathroom, no longer rules the buyer. New and more comfortable tub shapes and sizes are available in an array of colors. Most major manufacturers make tubs for the three types of installation: recessed, platform, and corner. Tubs can be purchased in whirlpool models and with grab bars and slip-resistant surfaces for safety. A white tub without special features is still the least expensive. Cost is affected by shape, size, material, color, and special features. Tubs are made of fiberglass-reinforced plastic, acrylic, synthetic marble, enameled cast iron (the heaviest), and enameled steel.

Styles	Characteristics
Rectangular 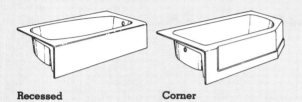 Recessed Corner	Rectangular tubs come in two styles: recessed and corner. Recessed tubs fit between two side walls and against a back wall; they have one finished side. Corner models have one finished side and end and may be right or left-handed. Interiors are rectangular or oval.
Square & receptor 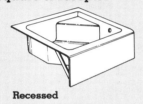 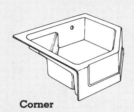 Recessed Corner	Square tubs are commonly 4 by 3½ or 4 feet; often they include an integral seating ledge. The difference between square and receptor tubs is depth. Receptors are usually only 12 inches deep—convenient for bathing children. You also can use a receptor in place of a shower base. Both square and receptor styles are available for recessed or corner installation.
Platform/sunken 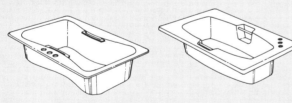	Platform/sunken tubs, most commonly available in fiberglass, enameled cast iron, or acrylic, are either set in a raised platform or sunk in the floor. Extra framing is often needed, especially for installation on an upper floor. Interior shapes and features vary.
Soaking  	Soaking tubs, like Japanese *furos* made of wood, have deep interiors. Ideal for use in small spaces, they're available in recessed, platform, and corner models with rectangular or round interiors. Those with round interiors often have a seating ledge. Fiberglass and acrylic are most readily available.
Special   Whirlpool Clawfoot	Whirlpool, clawfoot, and other special tubs allow you to slide into the lap of luxury. Many styles, including whirlpools, are made for two people. Because of their weight, larger tubs require special framing. They also may require an extra-capacity water heater and will probably increase your water heating costs. Not surprisingly, these are more expensive than other tubs.

FITTINGS FOR FIXTURES

Fittings are sold separately from fixtures. Select fittings that are easy to operate and durable. Fittings are priced according to materials, quality, and design.

Fittings for sinks are available with single, center-set, or spread-fit controls. A single-control fitting has a combined faucet and lever or knob that controls water flow and temperature. A center-set control has separate hot and cold water controls and a faucet, all mounted on a base. A spread-fit control has separate hot and cold water controls and a faucet, each independently mounted. Pop-up or plug stoppers are sold separately or with the faucet and water controls.

Decide which kind of control you want and then make sure it fits the sink. The number of holes in the sink and the distances between them—either 4, 6, or 8 inches—determine which fittings can be used. If fittings are to be attached to the wall or counter, the hole arrangement can be designed to suit the fittings.

For tubs and tub/showers, you can use either single or separate controls. Tubs also require a spout and drain. Tub/showers need a spout, shower head, diverter valve, and drain. Water-saver shower heads are readily available. You can purchase single-control fittings with pressure balancing and thermostatic valves.

The best fittings are made of brass and come in several finishes, including chrome, pewter, and gold.

Styles

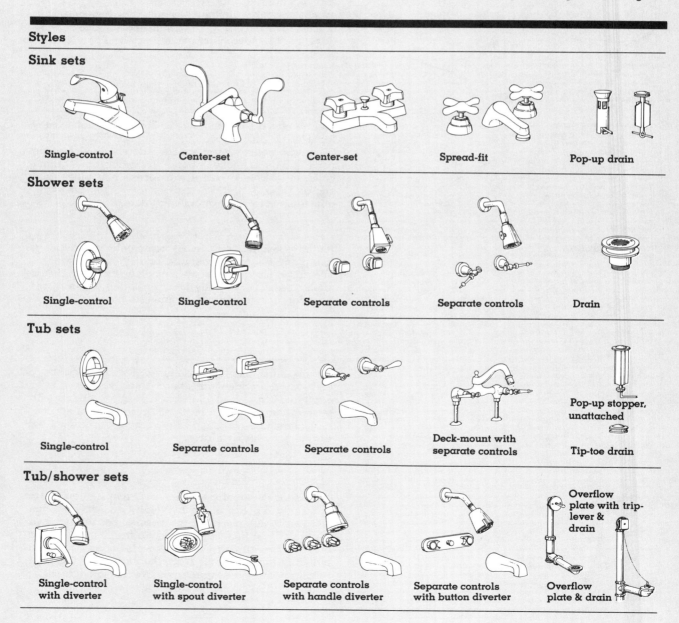

Sink sets

Single-control   Center-set   Center-set   Spread-fit   Pop-up drain

Shower sets

Single-control   Single-control   Separate controls   Separate controls   Drain

Tub sets

Single-control   Separate controls   Separate controls   Deck-mount with separate controls   Pop-up stopper, unattached   Tip-toe drain

Tub/shower sets

Single-control with diverter   Single-control with spout diverter   Separate controls with handle diverter   Separate controls with button diverter   Overflow plate with trip-lever & drain   Overflow plate & drain

TOILETS & BIDETS

Toilets vary in style, size, shape, installation, and flushing action. The flushing actions result from bowl design and vary in noise generated and in efficiency. When you select a toilet, first consider what kind of flushing action you prefer: washdown, reverse trap, siphon jet, siphon action, or up-flush.

Washdown toilets, no longer accepted by many code authorities, are the least expensive, least efficient, and most noisy. Less noisy is a reverse trap toilet, which is next in cost; it has a smaller water area, water seal, and trapway than the washdown or siphon jet.

More costly than the previous two styles, a siphon jet toilet is quieter and has a larger water surface; because it has a larger trapway, it is less likely to clog. Most expensive, most efficient, and quietest is the siphon action toilet, available only in a one-piece unit; its bowl interior offers the largest water surface. Up-flush toilets are used in basements when the sewer is above the floor level.

Water-saver toilets, designed with small tanks and shallow traps, use about one-third less water than conventional toilets—without a loss of efficiency. They're available in floor-mount, wall-hung, one-piece, and two-piece styles. These toilets have either reverse trap or siphon vortex flushing. Water-savers cost no more to install than conventional toilets.

A bidet, best installed next to the toilet, is floor-mounted and plumbed with hot and cold water. It is used primarily for personal hygiene.

Toilets and bidets are made of vitreous china.

Styles	Characteristics
One-piece  Floor-mount Wall-hung	One-piece toilets are characterized by their low profile, usually 19 to 26 inches high. These units are designed for floor and wall mounting. Available with round or elongated bowls, one-piece toilets have reverse trap, siphon jet, or siphon action flushing. Their design, efficiency, and easy installation make them a popular choice.
Two-piece  Standard  Safety  Corner  Back outlet	Two-piece toilets come in many models and can be mounted on the floor or on the wall (not shown). A wall-hung toilet, available only in siphon jet and siphon action models, offers easy access to the floor for cleaning. If you don't already have a wall-hung toilet, you'll face fairly major alterations to the wall framing and the floor. If you have special needs, consider special toilet designs. With its triangular tank, a corner toilet is a good choice when space is limited. The rim of a higher-seat safety toilet is 18 inches above the floor, compared to the 14-inch height of a conventional bowl. A back-outlet toilet has an above-floor drain. It's most frequently used on concrete floors, where it would be difficult and costly to install other toilets or relocate an existing one.
Bidets Center-fit  Spread-fit	Available with wall-mount or deck-mount water controls, a bidet comes with a spray spout or a vertical spray located in the center of the bowl. Some have rim jets for rinsing, to maintain bowl cleanliness. Most models also have a pop-up stopper that allows the unit to double as a foot bath or as a basin for washing clothes.

LIGHT FIXTURES

There are three main kinds of lighting: task, accent, and ambient or general. Task lighting plays an important role in the bathroom, where visual activities such as applying makeup, shaving, and reading take place. Accent lighting is similar to task lighting—it focuses light and attention on architectural features or sets a mood. Ambient lighting provides a soft, pleasing level of light, sufficient for such activities as taking a bath.

Many different kinds of fixtures can be used to achieve the kind and level of lighting you want in the bathroom. Because of the danger of electrical shock, bath and shower fixtures must be installed in recessed vaporproof housings. For more information about lighting, see page 30.

Styles	Characteristics
Built-in 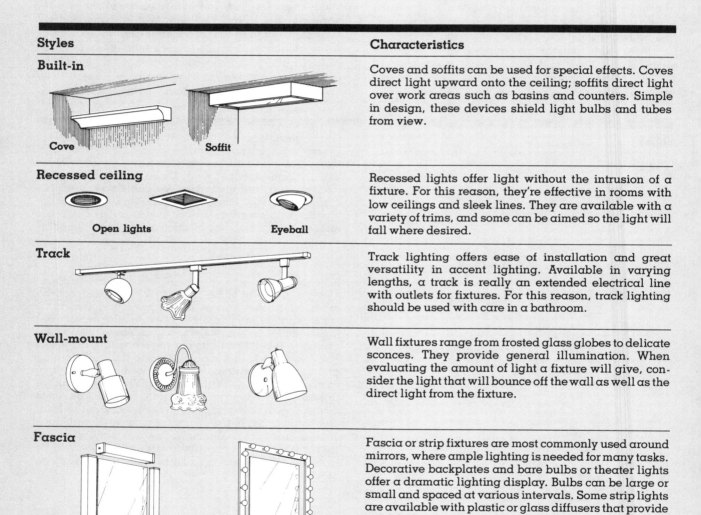 Cove Soffit	Coves and soffits can be used for special effects. Coves direct light upward onto the ceiling; soffits direct light over work areas such as basins and counters. Simple in design, these devices shield light bulbs and tubes from view.
Recessed ceiling Open lights Eyeball	Recessed lights offer light without the intrusion of a fixture. For this reason, they're effective in rooms with low ceilings and sleek lines. They are available with a variety of trims, and some can be aimed so the light will fall where desired.
Track	Track lighting offers ease of installation and great versatility in accent lighting. Available in varying lengths, a track is really an extended electrical line with outlets for fixtures. For this reason, track lighting should be used with care in a bathroom.
Wall-mount	Wall fixtures range from frosted glass globes to delicate sconces. They provide general illumination. When evaluating the amount of light a fixture will give, consider the light that will bounce off the wall as well as the direct light from the fixture.
Fascia	Fascia or strip fixtures are most commonly used around mirrors, where ample lighting is needed for many tasks. Decorative backplates and bare bulbs or theater lights offer a dramatic lighting display. Bulbs can be large or small and spaced at various intervals. Some strip lights are available with plastic or glass diffusers that provide a soft light.
Ceiling-mount 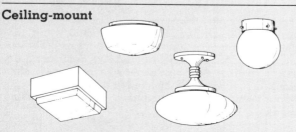	Ceiling light fixtures vary in style, but they're usually fastened to the electrical box mounted in the ceiling. They provide good general light in bathrooms and can be used effectively with task and accent fixtures. As with wall fixtures, check to see that the direct light from the fixture and the indirect light bounced off the ceiling is sufficient. If the room is large, you may want to consider a double or triple-globe fixture.

CERAMIC TILE

Ceramic tile is one of the most practical and popular surface materials for bathroom walls, floors, and countertops. Made of hard-fired slabs of clay, ceramic tile is durable, fireproof, mar-resistant, impervious to soil and moisture, and easy to maintain. It comes either glazed or unglazed, in deep and brilliant colors as well as pastels, and in a variety of shapes and finishes.

In glazed tiles color is applied to the surface before the tiles are fired at high heat. You can choose from several finishes: high gloss, satinlike matte, semi-matte, or dull and pebbly-textured.

Color runs throughout the body of unglazed tiles; natural clay colors or pigments are mixed with the clay prior to forming and baking.

Generally, ceramic tiles are made in three forms: floor tiles, wall tiles, and ceramic mosaics.

Floor tiles

Floor tiles are generally thicker than wall tiles. Their thickness makes them durable underfoot. Floor tiles come in squares, rectangles, hexagons, and octagons as well as Moorish, ogee, and other shapes (see below).

Unglazed tile has advantages for floor use: it's less slippery than glazed tile and shows wear less, since color extends throughout the body. If you plan to use glazed tiles on a bathroom floor, it's best to choose those with textured or matte surfaces for best traction and longest wear.

Floor tiles for bathrooms are classified into three general categories: glazed, quarry, and pavers.

Glazed tiles. A popular choice, imported glazed floor tiles are available plain or decorated, usually 8 inches square. Many have matte and textured surfaces.

Quarry tiles. These tiles commonly come unglazed, in clay colors, but they're available with colorful glazed surfaces as well. Thicknesses range from ⅜ to ½ inch; surface sizes vary from 6-inch squares and 4 by 8-inch rectangles to 12-inch squares. Rough and water-resistant, quarry tile is an ideal flooring surface both indoors and out. A variety of trim pieces are available.

Pavers. Like most quarry tiles, pavers are unglazed and water-resistant. These rugged tiles, available in many colors, come in three standard sizes: 4-inch squares (⅜ inch thick), 6-inch squares, and 4 by 8-inch rectangles (both ½ inch thick).

Wall tiles

Tiles in this classification are glazed and offer great variety in color and design. Generally lighter and thinner than floor tiles, they are used primarily on interior surfaces: walls, countertops, and ceilings. Their relatively light weight is a plus for vertical installation. The glazed surface is water-resistant, though the bodies are porous. Wall tiles can be used on floors if traffic is light.

Standard sizes for wall tiles range from 3-inch-squares to 4¼ by 8½-inch rectangles; thicknesses vary from ¼ to ⅜ inch. Other sizes and shapes are available. Many wall tiles come with matching trim pieces for edges, coves, and corners.

Wall tiles are also available in pregrouted panels—a handy shortcut that reduces installation time and effort. Designed primarily for tub and shower areas, a panel contains up to 64 tiles, each measuring 4¼ inches square. The panels have flexible, water-repellent grout.

Ceramic mosaics

Tiles sold under this name are generally small—2 by 2 inches or less. They come in sheets, mounted on thread mesh or paper backing or joined with silicone rubber.

Ceramic mosaic is one of the most colorful and versatile materials in the tile family. You can install it on curved surfaces, such as molded basins and arches.

Mosaics are made of natural clay tile or porcelain, the most vitreous tile material. Traditionally, mosaic tile was unglazed; color was added to the body.

Purchasing tile

Tile can cost from about $1 to $40 per square foot. Generally, the more tiles of a certain size, surface pattern, and glaze that are manufactured, the less each one will cost. Special surface treatments, such as glazing, texturing, and handpainting, cost more.

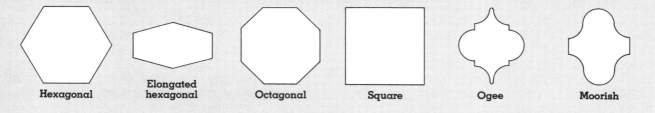

Hexagonal   Elongated hexagonal   Octagonal   Square   Ogee   Moorish

REFERENCE GUIDE TO BATHROOM MATERIALS

After being steamed, splashed, and sprayed, *good* bathroom materials still come up shining. That's because they're moisture-resistant—or better yet, waterproof. These materials are also durable—they wear well and are less likely to scratch, chip, stain, or scorch.

Described below are some of the materials most commonly found in the bathroom and those used in the manufacture of fixtures, including enameled cast iron, enameled steel, and vitreous china—mainstays in bathroom fixtures. Use this information to guide your selection of what's right for your bathroom, but don't hesitate to do a little investigating on your own.

It's a good idea to pick up product literature—available at showrooms, from dealers, or through manufacturers. If you have questions about products and materials, ask a salesperson.

Acrylic is more durable than fiberglass-reinforced plastic. It's thicker and has a higher gloss surface. Acrylic is chip and scratch-resistant, lightweight, easy to clean, and moderately priced. Many colors are available, and color runs throughout the material. Uses: bathtubs, one-piece and multi-piece tub and shower combinations with wall surrounds, shower stalls, and shower bases.

Carpeting used in bathrooms should be short pile and unsculptured. Nylon carpeting is a good choice—it's washable and stain-resistant, and it holds up well in moist conditions.

Enameled cast iron is more expensive and durable than vitreous china or enameled steel, but is very heavy. Its enameled surface is easy to clean and resists scratches, chips, and stains. Uses: bathtubs, sinks.

Enameled steel is easy to clean. It's lighter and less expensive than enameled cast iron, and also less durable. Most readily available in white, tubs are noisy unless treated to muffle sounds; they are prone to denting. Sinks come in many colors.

Fiberglass-reinforced plastic is lightweight and moderately priced. It's easy to clean, chip-resistant, and durable. Many colors are available. Fiberglass has a shiny, gel coat finish; use a nonabrasive cleaner to maintain it. Uses: one-piece and multi-piece tub and shower combinations with wall surrounds; shower stalls; bathtubs.

Glass is the traditional glazing material for windows, skylights, and shower doors. Many types are available for windows, including clear, tinted, reflective, insulating, patterned, and stained glass. Your building department may specify the use of shatter-resistant safety glass—available in tempered, laminated, and wire-reinforced varieties—for use in shower doors.

Marble, elegant and expensive, is impervious to water and heat. But if mistreated, it will scratch, crack, chip, and stain. Marble is cold underfoot and slippery. Uses: floors, walls, and countertops.

Plastic glazing is available in clear, patterned, and tinted panels for use in windows, skylights, and shower doors. It's easier to work with and install than glass, but it isn't as cleanable and abrasion-resistant. Because it's shatter-resistant, plastic glazing or safety glass is specified for bathroom use by some building departments.

Plastic laminate is applied with adhesive to particle board or plywood countertops, cabinets, vanities, and walls. Low to moderate in price, it comes in many colors and patterns. It's susceptible to burns and stains; edges chip and the laminate scratches.

Pottery is used in basins and fittings. It commonly comes in earth tones, but can be custom sculpted and glazed. It's less durable than vitreous china and enameled cast iron. It's susceptible to chipping.

Resilient flooring, available in sheets and tiles, is made of polyurethane, vinyl, and rubber materials. It's flexible, easy to install, simple to maintain, and resistant to moisture and stains. You can choose from many colors, patterns, textures, and styles. Cost varies greatly.

Synthetic marble is durable and fairly heavy. It's easy to clean; you may be able to remove scratches, stains, and burns with light polishing. Many colors are available, including pastels and veined colors. Uses: bathtubs, integral bowls, countertops, and wall panels.

Vitreous china is a mixture of clay that's poured into molds, fired in a kiln, and glazed. It is heavy, comes in many colors, and is easy to clean. It is scratch, chip, and stain-resistant. Uses: sinks, toilets, and bidets.

Wood used in bathrooms should be finished with a sealant to protect it from water. Untreated wood is likely to decay, warp, discolor, and streak in the moist environment of most bathrooms. It's best not to use prefinished wood planks and tiles. If used, they should be sanded in place and sealed thoroughly. Uses: flooring, paneling, countertops, and vanities.

ENERGY-SAVING IDEAS FOR WATER HEATING

The average household of four consumes more than 26,000 gallons of hot water annually. Heating this water accounts for about 20 percent of the family's total energy demand, an amount second only to that used for central heating.

But there's a slightly silver lining; as utility bills rise, the potential savings from energy conservation also increase. You can stretch your energy budget by acting on some of the following suggestions.

Make your water heater more efficient

Insulating or regulating your water heater can result in substantial savings on your utility bill.

Insulate the tank. Minimize heat loss by wrapping the tank in a special insulating jacket (see below).

You can buy a kit of fiberglass or foam that you can cut to fit around your gas or electric heater, or you can

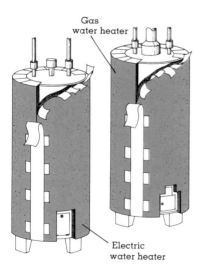

Gas
water heater

Electric
water heater

buy materials separately and make a jacket from scratch, joining the edges with sheet metal or duct tape.

Keep the insulating jacket clear of the pilot light and access panel of a gas heater or the pressure-relief valve of a gas or electric heater. Don't cover the top of a gas heater. Keep the thermostat and drain valve accessible.

Lower the temperature setting. In homes without dishwashers, reducing the water heater setting from the average 140° to 110° or 120° will save energy without making a noticeable difference in laundry or bathing.

Dishwashers, though, require 160° water. If you have a dishwasher, consider installing a tankless water heater to boost the water temperature to 160°. If you're buying a new dishwasher, you may want to choose one with a built-in booster (a tankless water heater).

Remember to turn down your water heater during vacations and other periods when your house will be empty.

Regular maintenance. You'll increase your water heater's efficiency if you maintain it regularly. Learn about sediment removal, proper adjustment of burners, and cleaning of heat transfer surfaces of gas units. For instructions, consult the manufacturer's directions or check with your local utility.

Install an automatic timer. You can program a timer to lower the thermostat of a gas heater or turn off an electric heater when usage is low. When more water usage is anticipated, the timer can raise the thermostat or turn the heater back on.

Insulate hot water pipes

To minimize heat loss from your hot water system, insulate all hot water pipes—especially those that pass through unheated or drafty areas. Several types of pipe insulation are available; the most common are polyethylene foam jackets that fit around most standard pipes and are fastened with tape. Another type of insulation is foil-backed, self-adhesive foam tape, which you spiral-wrap around the pipe.

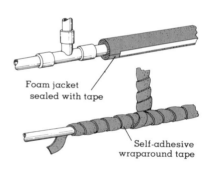

Foam jacket
sealed with tape

Self-adhesive
wraparound tape

Install an energy-saving water heater

If you're shopping for a replacement or supplementary water heater, look at energy-efficient models. Most heaters on the market today come with 2 inches of built-in foam insulation—more efficient than fiberglass, which it is fast replacing.

Solar water heaters are another energy-saving option. Capable of supplying up to 75 percent of your annual hot water needs, these heaters can almost always pay for themselves in less than 10 years. For more information on how you can heat water with the sun, consult a solar heating specialist.

Working with professionals

Major home remodeling projects are not easy work. Some you can do yourself; others may require some professional help. Still others are best left completely in the hands of professionals.

What jobs require professional assistance? How can you get the help you need? What is the best way to work with professionals? If you're confronted with questions like these, you'll find the following information helpful as you plan, organize, and carry out your remodeling project.

Do you need professional assistance?

The contribution you can make to your project depends on your knowledge, abilities, time, patience, and stamina. It also depends on local codes; in some communities, certain tasks involving structural, plumbing, and electrical alterations must be performed by licensed professionals.

If you know how to draw plans but dislike physical labor, you'll need to hire someone else to perform the actual work. Perhaps you're able to wield a saw and hammer but can't draw a straight line; you may need professional help only to prepare the new floor plan or specifications. Some people do the nonspecialized work, such as clearing the site and cleaning up later, but hire experts for everything else. Others let professionals handle the entire project—from drawing plans through applying the final touches.

In any case, you'll need to figure out exactly what you can and can't do as a planner and remodeler. Be frank with yourself about the skills you have and ones you're willing and able to learn. To help evaluate your skills, turn to pages 80–127; there you'll find step-by-step directions for remodeling tasks, as well as basic information about roughing-in plumbing, lighting, ventilation, and heating.

When you consult with professionals, be as precise as possible about what you want and about your budget (it's useless to have a spectacular set of plans for a bathroom you can't afford). Collect pertinent photographs, manufacturer's brochures, and advertisements. Describe the materials, fixtures, and fittings you want to purchase for the project—this is particularly important in bathroom remodeling, which often involves the replacement of expensive fixtures. Provide a drawing of your existing bathroom and sketches of your ideas. If you have questions, write them down before the interviews. The more information you can supply, the better job a professional will be able to do.

Architect or designer?

To help plan and design your remodeling project, you may want to consult an architect, a building designer, or a bathroom designer. Each can do the following:

• **Evaluate your remodeling needs** and design a project within your budget.

• **Draw preliminary sketches** and prepare floor plans—including details of structural, plumbing, wiring, and mechanical alterations—that will be acceptable to your building department.

• **Assemble necessary information** for contracts, detailing the work of each contractor or subcontractor.

• **Provide preliminary cost estimates** and specifications for bids.

• **Help you select** a contractor or subcontractors.

• **Supervise the contractor's performance** to ensure that your plans and time schedule are being followed.

• **Inspect the completed work** and prepare a certificate for final payment.

Not all architects and designers have the qualifications, experience, or desire to perform all of these tasks. Some designers don't have the technical background to plan plumbing and wiring changes; some architects prefer not to get involved with the construction aspects of the project. Some states don't require designers to be licensed, as architects must be; designers may charge less for their labor. If stress calculations have to be made, designers need state-licensed engineers to design the structure and sign the working drawings; architects do their own calculations.

Many architects are members of the American Institute of Architects (AIA), and many designers belong to the American Institute of Building Designers (AIBD). If you want to work with a bathroom designer, look for members of the National Kitchen and Bath Association (NKBA), a licensing agency for certified bath and kitchen designers. Each association has a code of ethics and a continuing education program to keep members informed about the latest building materials and techniques.

Some architects and designers charge for preliminary interviews, some bill for this time only if they don't get the job, and some will give short introductory interviews without a charge. For working plans, you'll probably pay on an hourly basis. If, in addition to designing your project and preparing working drawings, you want an architect or designer to select a contractor and keep an eye on construction, plan to pay either an hourly rate or a percentage of the cost of materials and labor—10 to 25 percent is typical.

Other fee arrangements may apply in your situation; some professionals combine an hourly fee for a certain part of the project with a flat fee for another part. For a small project that doesn't involve complicated structural changes, you may be able to hire an apprentice or drafter working in an architect's or designer's office to draw working plans for you; plan to pay by the hour.

Descriptions of the services to be performed and the amount of the charges should be agreed on in writing in advance, to avoid expensive misunderstandings later.

Contractors

Contractors are responsible for construction and all building operations. Often they're also skilled drafters, able to draw working plans acceptable to building department officials.

Generally, contractors obtain and pay for required permits, fees, and licenses. They arrange and pay for all labor, equipment, water, power, and tools necessary for the job. Work performed by contractors must comply with the codes, ordinances, and regulations in effect in your community. Contractors usually maintain all liability insurance, including workers' compensation, personal injury, and property damage; owners are usually responsible for fire, vandalism, malicious mischief, and extended insurance coverage. You'll want to make sure these items are clearly defined before you sign a contract.

Bids. For a major remodeling project, you will probably want to ask contractors (and subcontractors) for bids. To compare bids for actual construction, submit your working plans and exact specifications to two or three state-licensed contractors. Include a detailed account of who will be responsible for what work. If the bids you receive don't meet all of your requirements, ask for revised estimates.

You may not always choose the least expensive bid; higher-quality work or a more amicable relationship with the contractor may be worth extra expense.

Contract price and payment schedule. When you engage a contractor's services, consider both the bid price and the schedule of payment. Each is negotiable and should be specified in the contract. These are the most common types of bid:

- **Fixed price.** The contractor submits a bid for the project based on the working drawings and specifications. The figure includes all costs (excluding changes that come up during remodeling) and the contractor's profit. Though you don't see the cost breakdown until you award the contract, this is usually a desirable arrangement: it protects you against both an unexpected rise in the cost of materials (assuming the contractor does the buying) and against the chance that the work will take more time, adding to your labor costs.

- **Cost plus.** You pay the contractor for materials and labor plus a fee, usually 10 to 20 percent of that total, for profit and overhead. This method doesn't put a lid on the project's cost—a serious drawback unless you have a lot of confidence in the contractor.

- **Cost plus with a maximum total.** You and the contractor agree on a maximum total price for the job; the price includes the contractor's fee. If the cost of the work is less than the maximum total price, the savings are divided as agreed between you and the contractor.

Two payment schedules are common: installment and lump sum. With installments, your payments will usually be based on specific work completed and on materials delivered to the site. If your contractor agrees to a lump sum schedule, you'll pay for the entire project on completion.

Contract. After you select a contractor, make sure your agreement includes the following items in writing: working drawings, material specifications, services to be performed, total cost, method and schedule of payment, time schedule, and warranty against defects. Products and materials should be specified as precisely as possible. It's a common practice to specify in the contract what services the contractor is *not* expected to perform.

Not only is the contract legally binding to both parties, but it also minimizes problems by defining responsibilities. Changing your mind after construction starts usually requires a contract modification, involving additional expense and delays. All substitutions and modifications (and their costs) should be put in writing.

Protection against liens. Under the laws of most states, anyone who performs labor or supplies materials can file a lien against your building if he or she is not paid, even if payment was your contractor's responsibility. If you sell your property while a lien against it is in effect, settlement will be required before the title can be transferred.

You can protect yourself against such liability in several ways: pay suppliers of labor and materials directly; receive evidence of such payment before making your final payment to the contractor; or require the contractor to post a performance bond of sufficient size to protect your property. (The bond required by the state might not be large enough to cover all claims against a defaulting contractor.)

Hiring subcontractors

When you act as your own general contractor and put various parts of your project out to bid with subcontractors (plumbers, tile setters, electricians), you must use the same care you'd exercise in hiring a general contractor.

Check references, financial resources, and insurance coverage of a number of subcontractors. Once you've received bids and chosen your subcontractor, you should work out a detailed contract for each job and carefully supervise all work. Though this process will be time-consuming, you may save money and you'll have more control over the quality of the work.

The services of subcontractors include supplying current product information, selling products and materials, advising you, and doing the work in accordance

... Working with professionals

with technical drawings and specifications that comply with code. Subcontractors usually provide the tools and equipment necessary to complete the job.

Hiring workers

Even when you're operating as your own contractor and hiring subcontractors, you may want to hire additional workers on an hourly basis for their specialized skills or their brawn.

If you hire such help, you will have to provide workers' compensation insurance to cover possible job-related injuries. Though provisions vary from state to state, compensation insurance usually reimburses the worker for wages lost and for the cost of medical treatment. Policies are available from insurance brokers, insurance companies, and sometimes from state funds.

When you employ people directly and they earn more than a minimum amount set by the state, you must register with the state and federal governments as an employer. You will be required to withhold and remit state and federal income taxes; withhold, remit and contribute to Social Security; and pay state unemployment insurance. For more information, talk to a building department official, or check the subheading "Taxes" under your state listing in the white pages of your telephone directory.

For interior design

You may want to call on an interior designer for finishing touches. (If you work with a bathroom designer, decorative services will probably be included in the job.) These experts, specializing in the decoration and furnishing of rooms, can offer fresh, innovative ideas and advice, and through their contacts, a homeowner has access to products and materials not available at the retail level.

An interior designer could help you choose a new color scheme, shop for unusual accessories, or track down a hard-to-find fabric for curtains. And you might want to rely on such a professional to suggest ways to display luxurious towels, humidity-loving plants, or a favorite piece of art.

Interior designers work on an individual basis. Their approaches differ, depending on the type and size of the project. A preliminary interview is customary to discover whether client and designer can work together effectively.

Many designers belong to the American Society of Interior Designers (ASID), a professional organization. Expect to be charged an hourly fee or a percentage of the cost of all merchandise purchased for the project.

Where to look for assistance

The best way to find competent architects, designers, contractors, and other workers is by recommendation

from friends and neighbors who have used professionals in a project similar to yours. You can also seek referrals from retail building materials outlets.

The Yellow Pages list design professionals under "Architects," "Building Designers," "Interior Decorators and Designers," or "Drafting Services"; look for contractors to handle a remodeling project under "Contractors—Alteration" and contractors for major projects under "Contractors—Building, General."

The Yellow Pages are also a good source for more specialized information, such as suppliers of flooring, carpeting, painting, and cabinetry.

Choosing professionals—a final note

Your home is an expression of your family's identity. Whether you're remodeling or adding a bathroom, you're embarking on more than just a construction project; you're creating a personal space. In choosing a professional, try to find someone who's not only technically and artistically skilled but with whom you and your family feel comfortable and compatible.

You don't want to consign your remodeling efforts to a professional who will ignore your ideas and impose his or her standards. You do want a person who will take your ideas seriously and bring an increased measure of knowledge, skill, judgment, and taste to the project.

Admittedly, it's difficult to tell beforehand how well any professional will work with you, but you should direct your attention to that subject as well as to technical ones when you make your choice.

Obtain at least three referrals for each job to be performed. Then call each individual or firm and briefly describe your project. At this point you may want to arrange a preliminary interview or ask the professional for the names and phone numbers of customers. Call several and ask how they feel about the person and the completed work; if you can, inspect the work—an on-site inspection is more valuable than looking at photographs and slides.

When you interview professionals, ask about their experience with your type of remodeling, and about their time availability, working procedures, and fees. If you're dealing with a large firm, be sure to talk to the person who would be handling the project.

Don't be tempted to make price your only criterion for selection; reliability, quality of work, and on-time performance are also important. The professional you choose should be well established, cooperative, competent, and financially solvent. Check bank and credit references to determine financial responsibility. Your local Better Business Bureau is a good source of information about a firm's or individual's business reputation. Local chapters of professional and trade organizations may also provide assistance. Such organizations can be especially helpful in directing you to professionals with particular areas of expertise. If your project involves custom work, these referrals can be invaluable.

Permits, costs & financing

After you've taken stock of your existing bathroom, drawn floor plans and elevations of desired changes, and explored the dazzling world of fixtures, fittings, and materials, you're ready to turn your design into a reality.

This is the time to decide how much of the job you're going to do yourself, and to learn how to deal with professionals (see pages 42–44). It's also the time to determine what local restrictions apply to your proposed remodeling, how much the total job will cost, and how you're going to pay for it.

Building permits

Check with your building department to find out which building codes relate to your remodeling project and whether permits are required.

You probably won't need a building permit for simple jobs such as replacing a sink or changing floor or wall coverings. But for more substantial changes you may need to apply for one or more permits: structural, plumbing, electrical, mechanical heating or cooling, and roofing.

Before you obtain permits, a building department official may need to see working drawings to ensure that your plans conform to local zoning ordinances and building codes. If the project is simple, written specifications or sketches may suffice. More complicated projects may require that the design and working drawings be executed by an architect, designer, or state-licensed contractor or engineer.

If you plan to do all the work yourself, you may have to sign an owner-builder release exempting you from workers' compensation insurance before receiving the permits. You don't need workers' compensation insurance if you hire a state-licensed contractor.

If you apply for the permits but plan to hire other people to help you with the work, you must show a Certificate of Compensation Insurance (see "Hiring workers," page 44 for more information).

For your permit you'll be charged a flat fee or a percentage of the estimated materials and labor. You may also need to pay a plan-checking fee.

If you're acting as your own contractor, you must ask the building department to inspect the work as it progresses. A contractor schedules these inspections as part of the job. The number of inspections required depends on the complexity of the remodeling. If you fail to obtain a permit or an inspection, you may have to dismantle the completed work.

Figuring costs

Start by making a realistic budget that covers all the supplies you'll need and the cost of any professional help you plan to employ to accomplish the remodeling process.

Large items, such as tubs, toilets, vanities, and flooring, are easy to remember. It's more difficult to keep track of little items, such as nails, glue, and wall switches, which can add a tidy sum to your bill. To estimate costs for products and materials, list the tasks you plan to accomplish and the tools, supplies, and materials you need to rent or buy for each task. Estimate the quantity of each item and add a little extra for unforeseen problems. Don't overlook that "extra." No matter how carefully you budget your project, most remodeling jobs end up costing more than anticipated. Make your list as detailed as possible.

After you complete the list, call stores, dealers, manufacturers, and suppliers to obtain prices. Do some comparison shopping. When checking on prices, find out if the items you want are in good supply, or how long you'll have to wait for delivery. You may wish to select alternatives to your first choices—it's a good idea to do this, because missing fixtures or important materials can delay the work and increase the cost of the project.

If you work with an architect, designer, or contractor, he or she will prepare the list. Professionals usually have access to a larger variety of products which they can buy at lower prices—and they supply their own tools. If your supplies and materials are included in the contract price, your contract should stipulate that the contractor is responsible for the condition of the goods, their proper functioning after installation, and the correct color, shape, size, and model.

Cost of materials is only part of the expense of remodeling; the other part is cost of labor. The more work you do yourself, the more you can cut costs. Many remodelers prefer to do as much of their own work as possible, so they can afford to buy the best products and materials. In addition to honestly evaluating your skills, though, also think of the time required to accomplish each task. Working only on evenings and weekends can stretch a job from weeks to months. When you decide whether to do the work yourself, consider the inconvenience of living for weeks with a partially dismantled bathroom.

Shopping for money

If you're like most homeowners, you'll finance your project by arranging a loan. But first, you must have working drawings and specifications, and complete, accurate cost estimates of products and materials. You'll need to present this material to the lending institutions you contact.

It's important to shop as carefully for financing as for any of your new bathroom materials. Some of the possibilities include borrowing against life insurance, retirement or profit-sharing funds, savings accounts, or stocks and bonds. Your home is one of your biggest assets; consider refinancing, or adding a second mortgage. Lending laws vary from state to state—check the details of these methods as they apply to your situation.

Finalizing your plan

Before you complete your remodeling plans, you must confront the realities of your budget and your abilities. You'll need to estimate costs for each phase of the project, and familiarize yourself with planning schedules and negotiating contracts (see page 43). Evaluate your skills and the time you have available to work on the project. Consider how professionals can help you. You can then use this information to help define the scope of the remodeling project and your involvement in it.

Chances are you'll need to adjust some of your remodeling plans. If your estimated costs exceed your budget, you'll want to explore ways to reduce expenses. Perhaps you can substitute more moderately priced products for your initial choices. A really substantial difference may prompt fundamental rethinking of your project; perhaps you'll have to put aside your plan to enlarge your bathroom and reroute the plumbing to meet your new layout. In this case, you'll have to develop a new and less expensive design. Often an architect or designer can suggest affordable solutions to the problem.

You should also review your design for flaws. Check your calculations and reconsider your priorities. If you feel uncomfortable about any part of your plan, try to define the problem and solve it before you proceed. Remember that it's far less costly to make changes on paper before you start than it is after the work is underway.

Drawing your new floor plan

The planning process culminates with the drawing of your new floor plan. It's the basis for the remodeling work, for the preparation of a master list of products and materials, and for getting any necessary building permits.

Draw the new floor plan in the same style as you did the existing floor plan (see pages 20–21). On the new plan, include existing features you want to preserve and all changes, such as new walls, partitions, doors, windows, skylights, light fixtures, electrical outlets, fixtures, cabinets, countertops, and materials. As appropriate, note the locations, dimensions, and types of these items on the plan (see drawing below).

For more complicated projects, the building department may require additional or more detailed drawings of structural, plumbing, and wiring changes. You also may need to show areas adjacent to the bathroom on the new plan, so building officials can see how the project will affect the use of your house. Elevation sketches are not required, but they'll serve as a helpful check in planning the work and ordering materials.

If you order the materials for your remodeling project, you'll need to compile a detailed master list. Doing this helps you to launch your work and to keep track of purchases and deliveries. When you start working, it serves as a reminder of the materials required for each part of the project.

For each item, specify the following information: name and model or serial number, manufacturer, source of material, date or order, delivery date, color, size or dimensions, quantity, price (including tax and delivery charge), and second choice.

Reviewing your work

After you draw your new floor plan, review the tasks you've completed. Use the check list below to make sure you haven't overlooked an important planning consideration. The sequence of planning can vary, of course, depending on the individual project, its scope, your knowledge, and the extent of work you'll do yourself, and how much you want or need professionals to do.

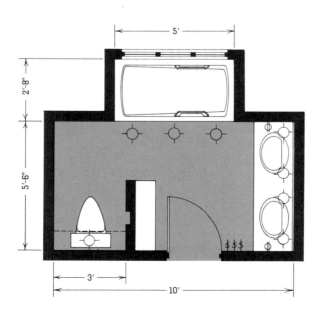

Your new floor plan—as well as elevations (not shown)—must clearly specify the proposed alterations, such as new walls, fixtures, and dimensions. The new fixtures in this floor plan are a 60 by 32 by 16-inch enameled cast-iron bathtub recessed in a cantilevered extension, a one-piece floor-mount toilet, and two oval self-rimming sinks set into a built-in vanity. Other new features include a partition storage wall with shelves and cabinets, a triple switch to operate groupings of recessed ceiling lights, and electrical outlets. This project would require a professional to prepare detailed drawings of structural plumbing, and wiring changes. The original plan is shown on page 21. If your project calls for simpler remodeling, you may need only to prepare a new floor plan and write the proposed changes on the plan. Key to the architectural symbols is on page 21.

Getting ready to remodel

Major bathroom remodeling can cause a mess and disrupt your household routine. You can take some steps now to minimize fuss and keep the house livable.

If water and electricity must be shut off, find out when and for how long during each working day. You'll want to know whether this will mean a loss of power and water just to the bathroom, to nearby rooms as well, or to the entire house. You may want to arrange in advance to have the use of a neighbor's bathroom during this time. If your bathroom will be exposed to the outside while remodeling is under way, you may want to protect the work area and the rest of the house from cold, heat, wind, and rain. Seal off the exposed area—wall opening, door, window—by taping heavy plastic sheeting over the opening. If security is a concern as well, nail sheets of plywood over the opening.

When a project requires demolition work, such as tearing down walls, taking up flooring, or removing wall tile, it creates a good deal of dust and debris. You don't want to trail this mess through the house. You can dispose of the rubbish through a bathroom window (you may want to build a temporary chute from the window to the ground). If the room doesn't have a window, you'd be wise to add tarps or plastic sheeting to your list of materials. You can use either to protect the floors and carpets, and you can tape plastic over doorways to help keep remodeling dust out of the rest of the house.

PLANNER'S CHECK LIST

First steps

____ **1.** Conduct bathroom inventory (pages 18–19)

____ **2.** Establish remodeling goals (page 19)

____ **3.** Measure bathroom; draw existing floor plan and elevations (pages 20–21)

____ **4.** Select architect, building designer, or bathroom designer (optional—pages 42–44)

Design

____ **5.** Determine bathroom style and start ideas notebook (page 22)

____ **6.** Study photographs for style ideas (pages 1–16 and 49–80)

____ **7.** Design your new bathroom (pages 22–25 and 28–30)
Consider basic design elements (pages 22–23)
Experiment with layout and clearance requirements (24–25)
Study sample floor plans (page 25)
Coordinate line, shape, and scale (page 28)
Choose a color scheme (page 29)
Plan improved lighting (page 30)
Draw new floor plan (page 46)
Look at "Bathroom showcase" (pages 31–40)

____ **8.** Have a professional check new floor plan, or have professional draw working plans and prepare specifications if desired—or if needed to obtain building permits

Permits, materials & contracts

____ **9.** Obtain building permits from building department, if needed (page 45)

____ **10.** Prepare products and materials list (pages 45 and 46)

____ **11.** Price products and materials (page 45)

____ **12.** Select contractor or subcontractors (pages 42–44)

____ **13.** Draw up contract (page 43)

____ **14.** Arrange financing (page 45)

____ **15.** Arrange for workers' compensation and other insurance, withholding tax, and Social Security contributions, if necessary (page 44)

Construction

____ **16.** Purchase products, materials, equipment, and supplies

____ **17.** Arrange for building inspector to check various stages of work at appropriate times (page 45)

____ **18.** Examine work daily and check to see that work schedule is being met

DESIGN IDEAS

Layouts · Lighting · Custom touches · Storage

Everyone knows a picture can be worth a thousand words, and that's the reason for this chapter. It's packed with full-color photos showing bathroom design ideas you can apply to your own situation, whether you're remodeling or starting from scratch.

The material is divided into sections. The first, "Open-plan baths" (pages 50–53), shows bathrooms with all functions organized in a single space—often a good decision when designing a master bathroom or one that's very small. The next section, "Compartment baths" (pages 54–57), deals with bathrooms planned for simultaneous use by more than one person, as often occurs in a family bath.

"Embracing the great outdoors" (pages 58–61) shows examples of bathrooms that open up to nature—sometimes literally, sometimes just to look at it. "Bright ideas" (pages 62–65), explores natural and artificial lighting—almost always subject to improvement when you're remodeling, and an important concern if you're designing a new bathroom. "Special tubs and showers" (pages 66–69) is a collection of stunning, even surprising, bathing facilities. "Custom touches" (pages 70–75) gathers a potpourri of large and small ideas that individualize a bathroom and make it special. And "Planning for storage" (pages 76–79) concludes the chapter with tips on making storage both generous and convenient.

Master-bathroom design concentrates wet areas in a single tiled corner beneath a glass hip roof. The shower doubles as a steam chamber. Architect: Bert W. Tarayao.

Open-plan baths

Logical extension
Silk-textured wall covering, sophisticated lighting, large mirrors, and a beautiful baroque washbasin highlight this distinctive, elegant design. Dressing counter, toilet, shower, and sink all share a single spacious room (below) that was added on to the bedroom (left). Since there's no intervening door, the bathroom functions as an extension of the bedroom. Architect: William Zimmerman.

Foreign stars
Imported Italian fixtures are sculptural focal points in this L-shaped master bath, which unites space formerly divided into two small bathrooms. The unit at center is a compact revolving cabinet. The owners laid the teak parquet floor themselves, sealing it with polyurethane.

Small package
Even tight spaces can contain complete facilities, especially when open planning is used. Here, a deep Japanese-style tub and a spray head on a flexible extension combine tub and shower functions in an area less than 3 feet square. Window openings were sized to fit standard greenhouse units; their shelves add storage space outside the wall. The double-basin counter provides still more. Continuous lines and coordinated finishes keep the number of design elements to a minimum and prevent the room from feeling too small. Design: Woodward Dike.

. . . Open-plan baths

F.O.B.
Like a shipment loaded and ready, the fixtures in this bathroom seem to be still in their crates. Built primarily of 2 by 4 framing lumber, the lighthearted open design features extensive roof glazing. Shades draw up if the sun becomes too intense. Architect: Douglas Kahn.

Presence of the past
This modern bath evokes the past in an abstract, almost symbolic way. Sinks, toilet, and bidet are arranged about the stencilled room in a series of "stations"; the shower and tub occupy a central peninsula. Design: American Standard. Stencil design: Ciel Lord.

Dazzling display

Expanses of mirror punctuated by clear lighting globes sparkle everywhere in this dramatic, open bathroom. The long counter combines vanity and platform tub in a single unit sheathed in blue plastic laminate. The room is an extension of the master bedroom. Children can enter through a doorway flanked by hot water pipes that act as a towel warming and drying rack. Pocket doors close off the space when needed. Architect: Edward Groder.

Compartment baths

Triple play

Three-room bath features a centrally located vanity compartment with tub and toilet in separate compartments at either side. Pocket doors allow private use by three people at once. The compartment at left houses a circular spa that doubles as a shower; the one at right contains the toilet, shelves, and a laundry chute. Wide mirrors and white walls make the most of light from a large skylight, keeping the room bright all day. A door at lower left leads to the rest of the house. Architect: Douglas R. Zuberbuhler.

Symmetry

Like the bathroom on the facing page, this one is divided into three compartments. Its outer area, open to an adjacent hallway, contains two vanities set opposite each other; each has a sink, a large mirror, and diffuse overhead lighting. Counters are clad in easy-care plastic laminate. The side-by-side inner compartments contain a greenhouse shower that shares its light through a glass door with the rest of the bath (below), and the toilet, which hides behind a mirrored door (right). Architect: Steven Goldstein/Environment +.

... Compartment baths

Lineup

Like the sections of a telescope, three progressively smaller rooms make up this linear design. Privacy increases as you move from the outer lavatory compartment into the drying area and finally into the secluded tub/shower. Glazed roof sections light all three compartments. In the lavatory area a ladder acts as a towel rack and leads to overhead storage for seldom-used items. Architect: Wendell Lovett.

Inner light

When a bathroom is divided into separate compartments, it can be difficult to provide daylight for the innermost one. This bathroom neatly solves the problem with a long skylight and a set of clerestories in the dividing wall. Each room shares light with the other; the inner one is always bright, and the bathing compartment beyond has light on its inside wall to balance the light of the exterior glazed wall. (Another view appears on page 58.) Architect: William B. Remick.

His and hers
She wanted a basin with a large counter, a big mirror, and lots of storage; he was
content with a sink, a medicine cabinet, and a shaving mirror. Both got what they
wanted. His modern pedestal sink is located in a daylit compartment that also contains
a tub/shower, toilet, and bidet. Her vanity takes up one wall of a smaller chamber
that has a large wardrobe on its opposite wall. Design: Sarah Lee Roberts.

Embracing the great outdoors

Private view, welcome light
A tiled platform runs right up to the sliding glass door in this master-bathroom bathing compartment (also pictured on page 56). The glazed wall provides a view of a private terraced garden and admits welcome light and air to a room that's on the dark, north-facing uphill side of a down-sloping lot. Indoor plants thrive in the humid air and indirect light. Architect: William B. Remick.

Double duty
This generous shower serves both the bathroom and a poolside deck. Large sliding glass doors on either side give access from inside and out, and present minimal barriers to the light. A refreshing shower alfresco is possible with the outer door open—and with the cooperation of Mother Nature. Architect: Edward Groder.

Bright mornings
Glass covers nearly the entire wall of this master bathroom stretched along the
southeast side of a custom home. Since privacy was not a problem, the entire space
was opened up to the light and the trees outside. It's a site-sensitive design: the
favorable orientation allows an early-morning warmup without the danger of over-
heating later in the day. Natural surfaces enhance the connection to the
outdoors. Architect: Donald K. Olsen.

. . . Embracing the great outdoors

Labor of love
A lot of work went into this custom tub/spa with its elegant beaded surface of wine red
mosaic tiles—and the results speak for themselves. Part of a master suite, the tub
alcove looks out through a butted-glass window to a private deck and a magnificent
view beyond. The tile was laid on a mesh-reinforced mortar base supported by
wooden framing. Architect: Marshall Lewis.

A little house of its own

This snug greenhouse tub steals a bit of space from the deck outside. A glazed roof allows romantic moonlit bathing by night and sunny soaks by day; mini-blinds assure any level of privacy desired. The tub is open to the master bedroom, which shares the light and view. The steel post carries structural loads. Architect: Rob Wellington Quigley.

A breath of fresh air

There's a view of the sea for users of this custom tub, and the casements open to welcome its breezes on warm days. The tiled tub is part of a wet-area design that also includes a shower—located away from the windows to ensure that the wooden frames remain dry. Architect: Chris R. Stephens.

Cool corner

Platform tub corners the view in this remodeling project. The cool tones of the tile and enameled tub/spa evoke a mood of serenity and relaxation. The tub doubles as a shower, with a partial shield of glass to control spray. Heat lamps are installed in a track above; mini-blinds are planned for extra privacy. Design: Rick Sambol for Kitchen Craft of Marin.

Bright ideas

Stepping lightly
Newly appreciated for their thermal efficiency and security, glass blocks have made
a comeback. In this elegant bath, blocks with differing surface textures create a
patterned stairway of light up one wall. Their grid effect is echoed in the mosaic tile of
the custom tub, far wall, and counter. The large mirror and recessed light fixtures
amplify the illumination. Architect: Marshall Lewis.

Light for the attic

European-made rotary windows are the keys to the daylighting scheme in this bathroom, part of a new master suite that took over the attic. The windows tip inward for ventilation and cleaning; rainproof vents allow air to flow in or out, but shield the room from water. Roller shades pull down when the sun becomes too intense. At night, more than a dozen lights provide balanced illumination. Architect: Glen William Jarvis.

A curving wall of light

A quarter-circle of glass block rounds out the inner corner of this L-shaped bath with abundant ambient light. A wall-wide mirror helps distribute the light, as do the tile, laminate, and white-painted surfaces. Ranks of incandescent bulbs brighten the vanity area. Architect: William B. Remick.

... Bright ideas

Multiple exposure

Mirror-lined corner picks up light from
the skylight in dressing room behind.
Recessed lights above the vanity provide
direct lighting. Together, they create
even illumination and an illusion of
greater space. The effect is enhanced by
the clean-lined cabinetry and cool gray
tile. Design: Rick Sambol for Kitchen
Craft of Marin.

A little more space,
a lot more light

This small bathroom grew a little,
physically—and even more,
visually—when a small greenhouse
"pop out" was added. Now the end wall
is nearly all glass (clear above, translucent below) and the added solar heat
keeps the bathroom cozy and dry all
year. Large casements open for ventilation. Architect: Larry Dennis Thompson.

Graceful gable

A frame of multiple arches opens up a gable-end wall; small panes within form a
neat grid. The design is a real attention-getter, but the window's beauty is more than
skin-deep—it floods the room with natural light and affords a lovely, private view into
the neighboring trees. Architect: William B. Remick.

Art and architecture

A large skylight illuminates this bathroom through a diffusing panel set in a wooden soffit. The design keeps light levels even and protects the valued art collection from direct sunlight. At night, fluorescent tubes in the light box produce the same omni-directional radiance at a lower intensity. The pre-Columbian figures can be lighted from below by a smaller light box set in the teak-and-marble vanity. Architects: Buff and Hensman.

Special tubs & showers

Time stands still
If the Victorians had thought of platform tubs, they might have built them like this, setting an old-fashioned rolled-edge tub in a stepped platform attractively sheathed in wall paneling. Since they didn't, this gracious old house had to wait more than a century before such a modern amenity could be included in its faithfully restored interior. Architect: Glen William Jarvis.

Eye opener
Here's a design to get you going in the morning: a greenhouse tub/spa and shower cloaked in burgundy tile, with white grout to emphasize their sculptural qualities. The bathroom shares its glass roof with a living room below; a glass wall and planting ledge separate the two spaces. Canvas shades pull up to beat the heat on sunny summer days. Architect: Bert W. Tarayao.

Restful retreat
The marble floor of this lofty bathroom steps down to become a sunken tub, and rises to become a low wall housing plumbing and dividing tub and vanity areas. The wide mirror reflects equally wide windows that look out on an adjoining flower garden—a view echoed abstractly in the large painting. The tub is the central element in a restrained and orderly design that tempers the luxury of fine materials and evokes a mood of quiet contemplation. Architect: Charles Moore. Bathroom designer: John Saladino.

. . . Special tubs & showers

Steam heat
Tattersall tile and a glass-block grid set the style for this large shower. Its dual nature is revealed when the sliding doors close and a steam jet in the built-in seat goes into action, converting the space into a steam room. Architect: William B. Remick.

Soaking in the view
This deep, circular soaking tub has hydromassage jets and a canyon view. It's installed in a five-sided bay added to an open-plan bath. Triangular clerestories flank the bay, flooding the room with light. Architect: Weston Whitfield.

An urban bower
A simple redwood platform encloses this square stainless steel tub set before large windows in a downtown loft. A hand-held spray head lets the unit double as a shower; cedar slats inside permit drainage and offer a warm seat. Abundant greenery adds a sylvan touch. Design: Vakavitch.

Stepping up
Handmade Mexican tile covers this large stepped platform with flush-mounted
fiberglass tub/spa. The curved notch at the back of the tub accepts a rolled-up towel
that acts as a headrest. The adjacent shower, lined with matching tile, is seen
through an etched glass window. Design: Diane Johnson Design.

Custom touches

Feminine finery

Tones of apricot, peach, and almond combine for a distinctly feminine look in this luxurious bathroom. Fine materials are used throughout: well-made plantation shutters, oak cabinetry, and marble for the bathing alcove and countertop. Architect: MLA/Architects. Interior designer: Stephen Chase.

Just for kids

Bright graphics, wall-wide mirrors, a space-saving receptor tub, and lots of ledges for the inevitable panoply of playthings make this small bathroom work hard for kids. Perimeter lighting and four centrally located ceiling fixtures keep things bright. Virtually every surface likely to get wet has been tiled—an excellent idea in a room that invites so much good clean fun. Architect: Douglas Kahn.

Incognito

Yes, it really is a bathroom. Camouflaged fixtures, and shelves filled with good reading material, give this master bath the character of a den or sitting room. It's actually a converted spare bedroom in a fine old Victorian house. The sink was built into an antique cabinet, the tub into a window seat; a toilet and shower hide in compartments behind the door and drape at left. The owners have occasionally used this gracious room as an overflow dining area when hosting large parties—a tribute to its truly chameleon design. Architect: Herbert D. Kosovitz.

Sunspot

This bathroom is planned as a nearly complete environment. An attractive step-down tub is set in a sunny window, and tanning lamps hang above a soft lounging platform for those winter days when the sun is only a dream.

. . . Custom touches

The spirit of bathrooms past
An authentic 19th century mood is evoked in this small guest bath. The new oak
vanity and handpainted sink harmonize with the antique mirror above; small lamps,
period-style hardware, brick floor, and old-fashioned wallpaper complete the picture. Architect: Weston Whitfield.

The spirit of bathrooms yet to come
This uncompromisingly modern guest bath would look at home aboard a starship
cruising some far-off galaxy in the distant future. But the imported tile and fixtures are
available today—right here on earth. Architect: Weston Whitfield

. . . Custom touches

From the potter's hand

Porcelain sink and matching tile display the fine craftsmanship and characteristic individuality achieved only when an object is handmade by one person. Here, both form and texture complement the cobalt-tinged glaze—it flows in the firing to reveal every change in level, from the stamped ducks in the medallion to the faint impressions of the canvas upon which the tiles were rolled.
Design: Kitty Purrington.

The carpenter's craft

This sleek mahogany basin appears to be an integral part of the single mahogany plank that makes up the countertop. Actually, it's formed from a series of pieces sawn to the rough profile of the sink, then laminated, carved, smoothed and fastened to the underside of the counter. Everything is finished with multiple coats of hand-rubbed spar varnish. Though not intended for heavy use, the extraordinarily elegant project is not unserviceable. And there is ample precedent for mixing wood and water: wooden boats have been with us for centuries. Design: Ron Helms.

Water sprite

This all-tile shower features a musical maiden sitting among lily pads. The tile picture "hangs" just above a built-in seat, where it helps to decorate not only the shower but the rest of the bathroom, too—a large space that includes the fireplace at left. (For a look at the accompanying tub, see page 66.) Architect: Glen William Jarvis. Mural: Brenda Rose.

Flights of fancy

Birds of paradise create a bit of heaven on earth in this bathroom. The design was handpainted on bisque tiles, then glazed and fired. Now the delicate painting shares the permanence of the stone-like tile of which it is a part. Design: Diane Johnson Design. Tile design: Barbara Vantrease Beall.

Planning for storage

Practical partner
Adding laundry collection to the usual duties of a bathroom often makes sense. Here, a modular European vanity shows off its capacious hamper that glides out beneath a synthetic-marble countertop. The vinyl-dipped wire sides and back help prevent moisture buildup. Design: European Kitchens & Baths.

Storage on parade
A row of standard steel medicine cabinets marches along the wall of this narrow bathroom in an impressive display of sheer capacity. Cabinets beneath the twin-basin countertop hold larger items in abundance. Greenhouse sections roof the room, filling it with light; they can be opened for ventilation. Architect: Peter W. Behn.

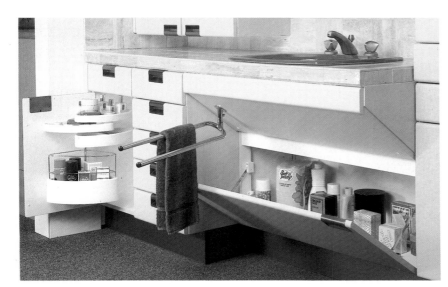

Large appetite

These German cabinets put away plenty in a surprisingly small space. Swing-out trays, stacked drawers, and an under-sink compartment that resembles an oversize automobile glove box are the keys to keeping everything sorted and out of sight, yet instantly accessible. Cabinets courtesy of European Kitchens & Baths.

Catchall

This handy cabinet pulls out on heavy-duty ball-bearing glides. One of its two plastic bins serves as a laundry hamper, the other as a waste basket. Beneath them, a shelf holds cleaning supplies and odds and ends. Architect: Michael D. Moyer.

Sky above, supplies below

Set in a grove of redwoods, this house was planned to take in the view from as many rooms as possible, including the master bathroom. With so much wall area given over to glass, there was a need to optimize storage below. The solution is this long vanity with drawer after drawer of well-divided, accessible space. In any bathroom, drawers are especially effective below counter height, since they eliminate the stooping and peering that can be a necessity with conventional cabinets. Architect: James K. Bell.

. . . Planning for storage

Private library
This handy redwood unit offers a magazine rack, a shallow cabinet, and a tissue holder all tucked into the awkward space between toilet and wall. Design: Marshall Design-Built.

Never give an inch
Every nook and cranny is a potential source of storage. Here, small drawers squeeze in between the toilet and tub; a large cabinet hangs above. The shelf atop the toilet hinges up for tank access, and two triangular tile shelves add convenience to the shower. Architect: Michael D. Moyer.

Inner space
Bifold louvered doors open to reveal a space-saving linen cabinet built through the wall in an attic bathroom. A shelf and a panel at the back of the cabinet lift out for access to the remaining attic beyond. Architect: William B. Remick.

Trompe l'oeil
Look carefully! It's all done with mirrors. Two stud-space storage compartments are built beneath the large mirror in this remodeled bathroom: the one at left is mirror-lined and open; the one at right lies behind touch-latched mirrored doors. Together they recover lost space and create little disruption in the mirrored wall. Architect: Ted T. Tanaka.

Bath and garden seem to grow together in this bright, verdant addition. The platform tub is partly shielded from the bedroom by an easily built half-height wall that lets the bedroom share the light of the new bay window. The knowledge of basic carpentry, plumbing, wallpapering, and tile work that this job required lies well within the reach of a handy homeowner. Design: European Kitchens & Baths.

REMODELING BASICS

Installation · Removal · Tools · Techniques

After sifting through a wealth of bathroom remodeling ideas, you've probably selected what's right for your family's special needs. Perhaps you've decided on a quick and easy change—a fresh coat of paint in your favorite color. Or maybe this is the time for the major remodel you've been dreaming about—moving a wall, opening the ceiling with a skylight, installing a gleaming new tub and surrounding tile.

This chapter is designed to help you translate your ideas and dreams into changes in your bathroom. From the basics of structural framing, plumbing, and wiring to the fine points of installing tile walls, it's all here for you to read and do. Each project begins with general information on planning and procedures, then takes you through the work with illustrated step-by-step instructions.

Though the directions assume that you have some basic knowledge of building terms, tools, materials, and techniques, you needn't be an expert to do most of the projects in this chapter.

Before work begins

Are you ready to remodel? Before plunging into a project, you should have a clear idea of the steps required to complete the job, and the sequence in which they should be done. You'll also need to evaluate your own ability to perform the various tasks. One of your first decisions will be whether to do the work yourself or get professional help.

Can you do the work yourself?

What skills do you need to remodel a bathroom? It depends on the improvements you're planning. Projects such as painting, setting wall tile, and installing floors and cabinets are within easy reach of any homeowner with basic do-it-yourself ability. You'll need a few specialized tools to complete some projects, but you can buy them at a building supply or home improvement center, or perhaps even rent them.

If you're unsure of your skills, consider taking some of the "how-to" classes available through adult education programs. These classes help you acquire experience without making a costly mistake in your home.

If your plans include complex remodeling projects such as moving bearing walls, running new drain and vent pipes, or wiring new electrical circuits and service panels, you may want to hire professionals to do part or all of the job. But many smaller structural, plumbing, and electrical jobs can be done by a homeowner with some basic experience.

Planning your project

Putting careful thought into your preparations can save you extra work and inconvenience later. As the scale of your remodeling project increases, the need for careful planning becomes more critical. If your home has only one bathroom, your goal is to keep it in operating order as much of the time as possible. With careful scheduling, the remodeling time will be easier for the entire family. As you plan, remember

to obtain any necessary permits from your local building department. If you're hiring a contractor, he or she will do this for you. But if you're doing the work yourself, you'll need to secure permits and arrange for inspections. Finally, before you start work, double-check the priorities listed below.

• Establish the sequence of jobs to be done, and estimate the time needed for completion.

• If you're hiring professional help, make sure you have legally binding contracts and schedules with contractors and subcontractors.

• If electricity, gas, or water must be shut off by the utility company, arrange for the cutoff date.

• Locate an area for temporarily storing fixtures that have been removed.

• Measure fixtures for adequate clearance through doorways and hallways, or down staircases.

• Locate a site for dumping refuse and secure necessary permits.

• Obtain all other required permits.

• Arrange for timely delivery of materials and be sure you have all the necessary tools on hand.

Note: If you're contracting the work, you can skip the last three steps; they're part of the contractor's service.

How to use this chapter

Reading all the sections of this chapter through quickly will help you to get a general feeling for what's involved in bathroom remodeling.

In the first three sections, you'll find an overview of structural, plumbing, and electrical systems. Even if you don't plan to do the work yourself, you may want to review these sections for background information. Understanding basic systems enables you to plan more effectively and to understand the reasons for code restrictions affecting your plans.

Many of your remodeling hours may be spent tearing out old work. To minimize the effort, we've included removal procedures along with installation instructions in the sections on fixtures, wall coverings, flooring, and cabinets.

If you're planning only one or two small projects, turn directly to the applicable sections for step-by-step instructions.

STEPS IN REMODELING

You can use this chart to plan the general order of removal and installation in remodeling your bathroom, though you may need to alter the suggested order, depending on the scale of your job and the materials you select. For more information, read the appropriate sections on the following pages. Manufacturers' instructions will offer additional guidelines as you go along.

Removal sequence

1. Accessories, decorative elements
2. Furniture, if any
3. Contents of cabinets, closets, shelves
4. Fixtures, plumbing fittings
5. Vanity countertops
6. Vanity cabinets, recessed cabinets, shelves
7. Flooring
8. Light fixtures, as required
9. Wall and ceiling coverings

Installation sequence

1. Structural changes: walls, door, skylights
2. Rough plumbing changes
3. Electrical wiring
4. Bathtub, shower
5. Wall and ceiling coverings
6. Light fixtures
7. Vanity cabinets
8. Toilets, bidets, sinks
9. Wall cabinets, shelves
10. Flooring
11. Accessories, decorative elements

Structural basics

Understanding your home's structural shell is a good way to begin any home improvement project, including bathroom remodeling.

Your house's framework probably will conform to the pattern of the "typical house" shown in the illustration below. Starting at the base of the drawing, you'll notice the following framing members: a wooden sill resting on a foundation wall; a series of horizontal, evenly spaced floor joists; and a subfloor (usually plywood sheets) laid atop the joists. This platform supports the first-floor walls, both interior and exterior. The walls are formed by vertical, evenly spaced studs that run between a horizontal sole plate and parallel top plate. The primary wall coverings are fastened directly to the studs.

Depending on the design of the house, one of several types of construction may be used above the first-floor walls. If there's a second story, a layer of ceiling joists rests on the walls; these joists support both the floor above and the ceiling below. A one-story house will have either an "open-beamed" ceiling—flat or pitched—or a "finished" ceiling. With a flat roof, the finished ceiling is attached directly to the rafters. The ceiling below a pitched roof is attached to joists.

Removing a partition wall

Sometimes major bathroom remodeling entails removing all or part of an interior wall to enlarge the space.

Walls that define your bathroom may be bearing or nonbearing. A bearing wall helps support the weight of the house; a nonbearing wall does not. An interior nonbearing wall, often called a partition wall, may be removed without special precautions. The procedure outlined in this section applies to partitions only. If you're considering a remodeling project that involves moving a bearing wall, consult an architect or contractor about problems and procedures.

How can you tell the difference in walls? All exterior walls running perpendicular to ceiling and floor joists are bearing. At least one main interior wall may be a bearing wall.

To determine whether the wall you're planning to move is bearing, climb up into the attic or crawlspace and check the ceiling joists. If they are joined over any wall, that wall is bearing. Even if joists span the entire width of the house, their midsections may be supported by a bearing wall at the point of maximum allowable span. If you have any doubts about the wall, consult an architect, contractor, or building inspector.

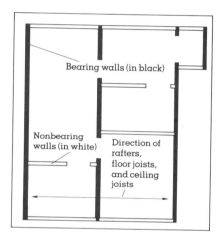

Bearing walls (in black)

Nonbearing walls (in white)

Direction of rafters, floor joists, and ceiling joists

Though removing a partition wall is not complicated, it can be quite messy. Cover the floors and fixtures, and wear a painter's mask, safety glasses, and gloves. NOTE: Check the wall for signs of wiring, water and drain pipes, or heating and ventilation ducts; you'll have to reroute them.

Remove the wall covering. First, if there's a door in the wall, remove it from its hinges. Pry off any door trim, ceiling molding, and base molding.

The most common wall covering is gypsum wallboard nailed to wall studs. To remove it, use a prybar (see "Removing gypsum wallboard," page 114).

If the wall covering is plaster and lath, chisel away the plaster and cut the lath backing—wood strips or metal—so that you can pry off the pieces of lath and plaster.

TYPICAL HOUSE STRUCTURE

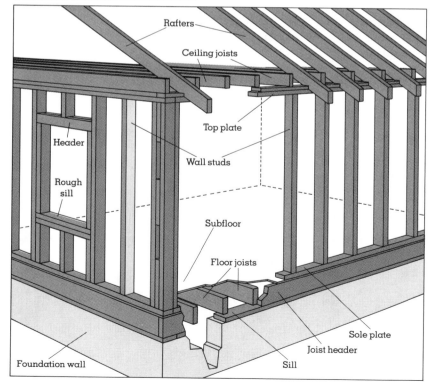

Rafters

Ceiling joists

Top plate

Header

Wall studs

Rough sill

Subfloor

Floor joists

Sole plate

Joist header

Foundation wall

Sill

(Continued on next page)

. . . Structural basics

DISMANTLING THE WALL FRAMING

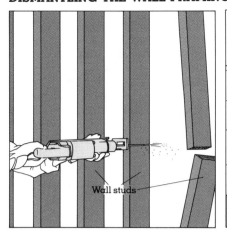

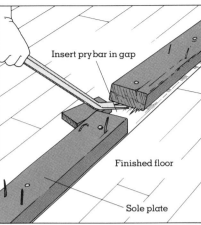

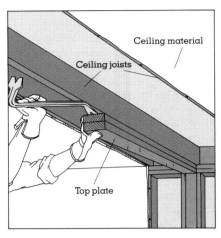

Saw through the middle of the wall studs; bend the studs sideways to free the nails from the top and sole plates.

Cut gaps through the sole plate with a saw and chisel; insert a prybar in each gap and lift to free the sole plate.

Strip ceiling materials back from the top plate, cut gaps in the plate, and pry out sections of plate.

Dismantle the framing. Remove studs by sawing through the middle of each one; then push and pull them sideways to free the nails (see illustration above).

To remove the sole plate, saw a small section out of the middle down to the finished floor level, chisel through the remaining thickness, and insert a prybar in the gap.

To remove a top plate that lies parallel to the joists, cut ceiling materials back to adjacent joists, and pry off the plate. If the top plate is perpendicular to the joists, you are probably working on a bearing wall and will have to take special precautions (see page 83).

Patch walls, ceiling, and floor. Wallboard and plaster aren't difficult to patch (see page 116); the real challenge lies in matching a special texture, wallpaper, shade of paint, or well-aged floor. This is not a problem if your remodeling plans call for new wall coverings, ceiling, or flooring. In either case, see the sections on "Wall coverings" (pages 114–121) and "Flooring" (pages 122–124) for techniques and tips.

Framing a new wall

To subdivide a large bathroom or to enlarge a cramped one, you may need to build a new partition wall or partial wall. Components of wall framing are illustrated below.

Framing a wall is a straightforward task, but you must measure carefully and check the alignment as work progresses. The basic steps are listed below. If you plan to install a doorway, see pages 85–86.

Plot the location. The new wall must be anchored securely to existing ceiling joists, the floor, and, at least on one side, to wall studs. To locate the studs, try knocking with your fist along the wall until the sound changes from hollow to solid.

If you have wallboard, you can use an inexpensive stud finder; often, though, the nails that hold wallboard to the studs are visible on close inspection.

To locate ceiling joists, use the same methods or, from the attic or crawlspace, drive small nails down through the ceiling on both sides of a joist to serve as reference points below. Adjacent joists and studs will be evenly spaced, usually about 16 or 24 inches apart.

WALL FRAMING COMPONENTS

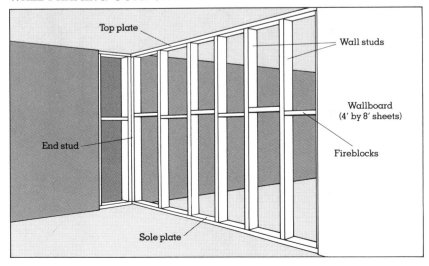

A wall running perpendicular to the joists will demand the least effort to attach. If wall and joists will run parallel, though, try to center the wall under a single joist; otherwise, you'll need to remove ceiling materials between two parallel joists and install nailing blocks every 2 feet (see illustrations at right). If the side of the new wall falls between existing studs, you'll need to install additional nailing blocks.

On the ceiling, mark both ends of the center line of the new wall. Measure 1¾ inches (half the width of the top plate) on both sides of each mark. Snap parallel lines between corresponding marks with a chalk line; the top plate will occupy the space between the lines.

Position the sole plate. Hang a plumb bob from each end of the lines you just marked and mark these new points on the floor. Snap two more chalk lines to connect these points.

Cut both sole plate and top plate to the desired length. Lay the sole plate between the lines on the floor and nail it in place with 10-penny nails spaced every 2 feet. (If you have a masonry floor, use a masonry bit to drill a bolt hole through the sole plate every 2 or 3 feet. Insert expansion anchors for lag bolts and bolt the sole plate to the floor.)

If you're planning a doorway (see "Framing a doorway," below), don't nail through that section of the plate; it will be cut out later.

Mark stud positions. Lay the top plate against the sole plate, as shown in the illustration. Beginning

ANCHORING A TOP PLATE

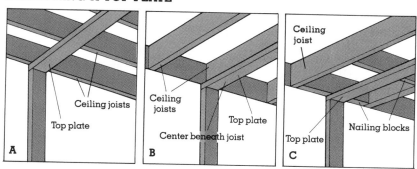

To anchor a top plate, nail to perpendicular joists (A) or to the bottom of the parallel joist (B), or install nailing blocks between parallel joists (C).

at the end that will be attached to an existing stud or to nailing blocks, measure in 1½ inches—the thickness of a 2 by 4 stud—and draw a line across both plates with a combination square. Starting once more from that end, measure and draw lines at 15¼ and 16¾ inches. From these lines, advance 16 inches. Don't worry if the spacing at the far end is less than 16 inches. (If local codes permit, use a 24-inch spacing— you'll save lumber—and adjust the placement of lines to 23¼ and 24¾ inches.)

Fasten the top plate. While two helpers hold the top plate in position between the lines (marked on the ceiling), nail it to perpendicular joists, to one parallel joist, or to nailing blocks, as shown above.

Attach the studs. Measure and cut the studs to exact length. Attach one end stud (or both) to existing studs or to nailing blocks between studs. Lift

the remaining studs into place one at a time; line them up on the marks, and check plumb with a carpenter's level. Toenail the studs to both top plate and sole plate with 8-penny nails.

Many building codes require horizontal fireblocks between studs. The number of rows depends on the code; if permitted, position blocks to provide an extra nailing surface for wall materials.

Finish. After the studs are installed, it's time to add any electrical outlets and switches (see pages 93–94), as well as any new plumbing (pages 90–91). It's also time for the building inspector to check your work. Following the inspection, you can apply wall coverings of your choice (see pages 114–121).

Framing a doorway

Your remodeling may call for changing the position of a door and creating a new door opening. Be sure the wall you plan to cut into is a nonbearing wall (see page 83); if it's a bearing wall, consult a professional.

Position the opening. This section assumes that you'll install a standard prehung door and frame. Build the rough opening 2½ inches wider than the door frame and 3 inches higher. These dimensions allow for the thickness of the finished frame (made of two side jambs and a head, or top, jamb), proper clearance

MARKING STUD POSITIONS

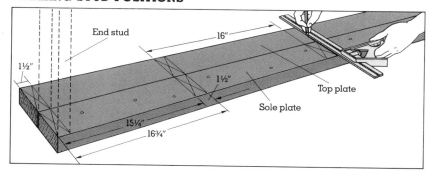

... Structural basics

between the door and frame, and space for shims between the door frame and the rough framing.

In addition, when removing the wall covering, be sure to allow enough room for the rough framing—one or more 2 by 4s on each side and the top.

Often it's simpler to remove the wallboard from floor to ceiling between two bordering studs (the new king studs) that will remain in place. (This is the method illustrated.) In any case, you'll save work later if you can use at least one existing stud as part of the new framing.

Regardless of the method you choose, use a carpenter's level for a straightedge, and mark the outline of the opening on the wall.

Remove wall covering and studs. First remove any base molding. Cut along the outline of the opening with a reciprocating or keyhole saw, being careful to cut only the wallboard, not the studs beneath. Pry the wallboard away from the framing. To remove plaster and lath, chisel through the plaster to expose the lath; then cut the lath, and pry lath and plaster loose.

Cut the studs inside the opening to the height required for the header (see illustration below). Using a combination square, mark these studs on the face and one side, then

cut carefully with a reciprocating or crosscut saw. Remove the cut studs from the sole plate.

Frame the opening. With wall covering and studs removed, you're ready to frame the opening. Measure and cut the header (for a partition wall you can use a 2 by 4 laid flat), and toenail it to the king studs with 8-penny nails. Nail the header to the bottoms of the cripple studs.

Cut the part of the sole plate within the opening, and pry it away from the subfloor (see "Removing a partition wall," page 83).

Cut trimmer studs and nail them to the king studs with 10-penny nails in a staggered pattern. You'll probably need to adjust the width by blocking out a third trimmer from one side, as shown below right. (Leave an extra ½ inch on each side for shimming, plus space for the door jambs.)

Hang the door. A standard pre-hung door and frame are predrilled for a lockset. The door comes already fitted and attached to the frame with hinges. Pull out the hinge pins to remove the door before you install the frame. Nail the frame in the rough opening, shimming carefully to make the side jambs plumb and the head jamb level. Rehang the

door and install the lockset; then install stop molding and trim (casing).

Closing a doorway

It's easy to eliminate an existing doorway. Simply add new studs within the opening and attach new wall coverings. The only trick is to match the present wall surface.

First, remove the casing around the opening. Then remove the door from its hinges or guide track, and pry any jambs or tracks away from the rough framing.

Next, measure the gap on the floor between the existing trimmer studs; cut a length of 2 by 4 to serve as a new sole plate. Nail it to the floor with 10-penny nails. (If you have a masonry floor, attach the 2 by 4 with lag bolts and expansion anchors).

Measure and cut new studs to fill the space; position one stud beneath each cripple stud. Toenail the studs to the new sole plate and header with 8-penny nails. Add fireblocks between studs if required by the local code.

Strip the wall coverings back far enough to give yourself a firm nailing surface and an even edge. Then add new coverings to match the existing ones, or resurface the entire wall (see pages 114–121). Match or replace the baseboard molding.

FRAMING A DOORWAY

Mark and cut studs within the opening to a height even with the top of the new header, and remove.

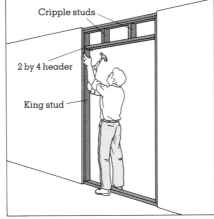

Nail the new header to the king studs, then nail through the header into the ends of the new cripple studs.

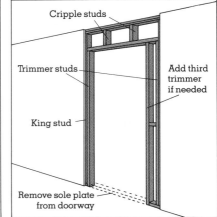

Nail trimmer studs to the king studs; add a third trimmer, if needed, to make the opening the correct width.

SKYLIGHTING THE BATHROOM

A skylight brings light and an open feeling into windowless interior bathrooms or those where uncovered windows would be a privacy problem.

Installing a skylight in a pitched roof with asphalt or wood shingles is a two-part process: you cut and frame openings in both roof and ceiling, and connect the two openings with a vertical light shaft. (You don't even need a light shaft for a flat roof or open-beamed ceiling.) A description of the installation sequence follows; for more detailed information, consult the manufacturer's instructions or your skylight dealer.

Mark the openings. Begin by measuring and marking the location of the ceiling opening. Then drive nails up through the four corners and center so they'll be visible in the attic. You'll save work if you can use one or two ceiling joists as the edges of your opening.

With a plumb bob, transfer the center mark to the underside of the roof. Mark the roof opening suggested by the manufacturer on the underside of the roof and drive nails through the corners.

Frame the roof opening. Exercise extreme caution when working on the roof; if the pitch is steep or if you have a tile or slate roof, you might leave this part to professionals.

If your skylight must be mounted on a curb frame, build the curb first; 2 by 6 lumber is commonly used.

To determine the actual size of the opening you need to cut, add the dimensions of any framing materials—headers, existing joists, and trimmer studs—to the rough opening size marked by the nails. You may need to remove some extra shingles or roofing materials down to the

BASIC PARTS OF A SKYLIGHT

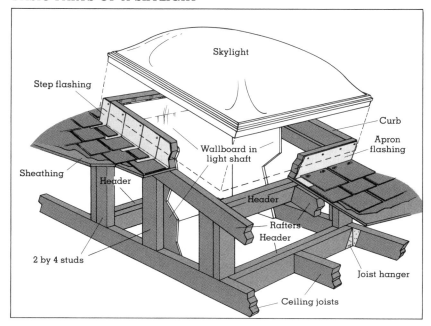

sheathing to accommodate the flashing of a curb-mounted unit or the flange of a self-flashing unit.

Cut the roof opening in successive layers: roofing materials first, sheathing next, and finally the rafters. Before cutting the rafters, support them by 2 by 4s nailed to the ceiling joists below.

Frame the opening as illustrated above, installing the headers with double joist hangers.

If you're installing a curb-mounted unit, position and flash the curb. Toenail the curb to the rafters or trimmers and to the headers. Flash according to the manufacturer's instructions.

Mount the skylight. For a curb-mounted unit, secure the skylight to the top of the curb with nails and a sealant. Nail a self-flashing unit

through the flange directly to the roof sheathing; then coat the joints and nail holes with roofing cement.

Open the ceiling. Cut through the ceiling materials and then cut the joists. Support joists to be cut by bracing them against adjacent joists. Frame the opening in the manner used for the roof opening.

Build a light shaft. Measure the distance between the ceiling headers and roof headers at each corner and at 16-inch intervals between the corners. Cut studs to fit the measurements and install them as illustrated above. This provides a nailing surface for wall coverings.

To finish, insulate the spaces between studs in the light shaft before fastening wall coverings to the studs. Trim the ceiling opening with molding strips.

Plumbing basics

Whether you're planning to add a single fixture or remodel an entire bathroom, you'll need an introduction to plumbing basics. Replacing an old bathtub, sink, or toilet with a new one at the same location is a straightforward job, but roughing-in (installing) plumbing for fixtures at new locations takes skill and planning.

What follows is an overview of fundamentals—household plumbing systems, plumbing codes, and general procedures for planning, routing, and roughing-in new pipes. This information may help you to decide whether to make your project a do-it-yourself effort or a professional one. If you have doubts, consider a compromise—you might hire a professional to check your plans and install pipes, then make the fixture hookups yourself (see pages 98–113).

If you want to do all the work yourself, read the information that follows before you begin to ensure that you're familiar with the tools and techniques required for the job.

How the system works

Three complementary sets of pipes work together to fill your home's plumbing needs: the water supply system, and the drain-waste and vent (DWV) systems (see the illustration below).

The supply system. Water for your toilet, tub, shower, and sink enters the house from a public water main or from a source on the property. Water from a water company is usually delivered through a water meter and a main shutoff valve. You'll find the meter either in your basement or crawlspace, or outdoors, near your property line. The main shutoff valve—which turns the water for the whole house on and off—is usually situated near the water meter.

At the water service entrance, the main supply line divides in two—one line branching off to be heated by the water heater, the other remaining as cold water. The two pipes usually run parallel below the first-floor level until they reach the vicinity of a group of fixtures, then

head up through the wall or floor. Sometimes the water supply—hot, cold, or both—passes through a water softener or filter before reaching the fixtures.

Supply pipes are installed with a slight pitch in the runs, sloping back toward the lowest point in the system so that all pipes can be drained. Sometimes at the lowest point there's a valve that can be opened to drain the system—essential for vacation homes in cold climates.

Drain-waste and vent systems. The drain-waste pipes take advantage of gravity to channel waste water and solid wastes to the house sewer line. Vent pipes carry away sewer gas and maintain atmospheric pressure in drainpipes and fixture traps. The traps (curved sections in the fixtures' drainpipes) remain filled with water at all times to keep gases from coming up the drains.

Every house has a 3 or 4-inch-diameter main soil stack that serves a dual function. Below the level of the fixtures, it is your home's primary drainpipe; above the stack it becomes a vent with its upper end protruding through the roof. Drainpipes from individual fixtures, as well as branch drains, connect to the main stack. These pipes lead away from all fixtures at a carefully calculated slope—normally ¼ inch per foot. Since any system may clog now and then, cleanouts usually are placed at the upper end of each horizontal section of drainpipe.

A fixture or fixture group located on a branch drain far from the main stack will have a secondary vent stack of its own rising to the roof.

Planning and layout

This section outlines the planning process and explores some of your options in adding new plumbing. When plotting out any plumbing addition you must balance code restrictions, the limitations of your system's layout, design considerations, and, of course, your own plumbing abilities.

A PLUMBING OVERVIEW

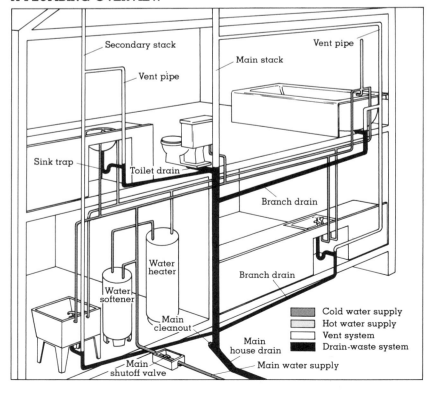

Secondary stack
Vent pipe
Main stack
Vent pipe
Sink trap
Toilet drain
Branch drain
Water heater
Branch drain
Water softener
Main cleanout
Main house drain
Main shutoff valve
Main water supply

Cold water supply
Hot water supply
Vent system
Drain-waste system

Check the codes. Almost any improvement that adds pipe to the system will require approval from local building department officials before you start, and inspection of the work before you close the walls and floor.

Learn what work you may do yourself—some codes require that certain work be done only by licensed plumbers.

Map your system. A detailed map of your present system will give you a clear picture of where it's feasible to tie into supply and drain lines, and whether the present drains and vents are adequate for the use you plan.

Starting in the basement, sketch in the main soil stack, branch drains, house drain, and accessible cleanouts; then trace the networks of hot and cold supply pipes. Also, check the attic or roof for the course of the main stack and any secondary vent stacks. Determine and mark on the sketch the materials and, if possible, the diameters of all pipes (see "Materials," at right).

Layout options. Plan the plumbing for any new fixtures in three parts: supply, drainage, and venting. To minimize cost and keep the work simple, arrange a fixture or group of fixtures so they are as close to the present pipes as possible.

Three economical ways to group your new fixtures (see drawings below) are to:

• connect an individual fixture to the existing stack (drawing A)

• add a fixture or group above or below an existing group on the stack

• tie a fixture (except a toilet) directly into a new or existing branch drain (drawing B)

If your addition is planned for an area across the house from the existing plumbing, you'll probably need to run a new secondary vent stack up through the roof, and a new branch drain to the soil stack (see drawing B below) or to the main house drain via an existing cleanout.

The new vent stack must be installed inside an existing wall (a big job), built into a new oversize or "thickened" wall (see "Build a wet wall," page 90), or concealed in a closet or cabinet. In mild climates, a vent may also run up the exterior of the house, but it must be hidden within a box.

Materials. Decide what kind of pipe you'll need, based on the material of the pipe you'll be tying into.

Your home's supply pipes most likely are either galvanized steel (referred to as "galvanized" or "iron"

pipe) connected by threaded fittings, or rigid copper joined with soldered fittings.

Your present DWV pipes probably are made of cast iron, with "hub" or "bell-and-spigot" ends joined by molten lead and oakum. (DWV pipes other than the main stack may be galvanized.)

To extend cast-iron pipes, you may substitute "hubless" fittings (consisting of neoprene gaskets and stainless steel clamps), which are simpler to install than hub fittings.

If you wish to change pipe material in your extension, it's a matter of inserting the appropriate adapter at the fitting end. You might want to change cast-iron or galvanized pipe to copper or plastic pipe. First check your local code, because some areas prohibit use of plastic pipe.

Plumbing codes

Few code restrictions apply to simple extensions of hot and cold water supply pipes, provided your house's water pressure is up to the task. The material and diameter for supply pipes serving each new fixture or appliance are spelled out clearly in the plumbing code. More troublesome are the pipes that make up the DWV system. Codes are quite specific about the following: the size of stacks, drainpipes, and vents serving any new fixture requiring drainage; the critical distance from fixture traps to the stack; and the method of venting fixtures.

Stack, drain, and vent size. The plumbing code will specify minimum diameters for stacks and vents in relation to numbers of *fixture units.* (One fixture unit represents 7.5 gallons or 1 cubic foot of water per minute.) In the code you'll find fixture unit ratings for all plumbing fixtures given in chart form.

To determine drainpipe diameter, look up the fixture or fixtures you're considering on the code's fixture unit chart. Add up the total fixture units; then look up the drain diameter specified for that number of units.

PLUMBING LAYOUT OPTIONS

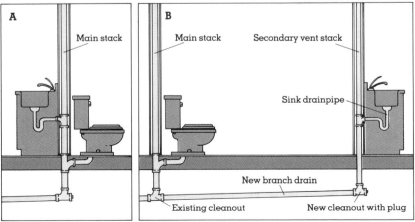

To drain bathroom plumbing additions, you can either (A) tap into the present main stack, if nearby, or (B) install a new branch drain and secondary vent stack.

(Continued on next page)

. . . Plumbing basics

Vent pipe sizing criteria also include *length* of vent and *type* of vent, in addition to fixture unit load.

Critical distance. The maximum distance allowed between a fixture's trap and the stack or main drain that it empties into is called the critical distance. No drain outlet may be completely below the level of the trap's crown weir (see illustration below)—if it were, it would act as a siphon, draining the trap. Thus, when the ideal drainpipe slope of ¼ inch per foot is figured in, the length of that drainpipe quickly becomes limited. But if the fixture drain is *vented* properly within the critical distance, the drainpipe may run on indefinitely to the actual stack or main drain.

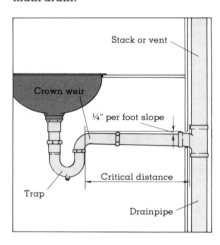

Venting options. The four basic venting options (see illustration above right)—subject to local code—are wet venting, back venting, individual venting, and indirect venting.

• *Wet venting* is simplest—the fixture is vented directly through the fixture drain to the soil stack.

• *Back venting (reventing)* involves running a vent loop up past fixtures to reconnect with the main stack or secondary vent above the fixture level.

• *Individual (secondary) venting* means running a secondary vent stack up through the roof for a new fixture or group of fixtures distant from the main stack.

VENTING OPTIONS

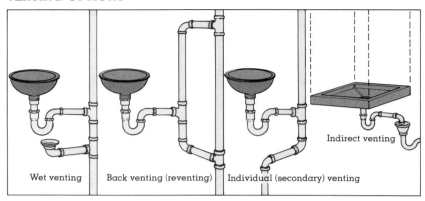

Wet venting   Back venting (reventing)   Individual (secondary) venting   Indirect venting

• *Indirect venting* allows you to vent some fixtures (such as a basement shower) into an existing floor drain or laundry tub without further venting.

Roughing-in new plumbing

Once you've planned your plumbing additions, you can begin installation.

Locate and tie into existing pipe. In the mapping stage, you determined the rough locations of the pipes. The next step is to pinpoint them and cut away wall, ceiling, or floor coverings along studs or joists to expose the sections you want to tie into. Be sure to cut out holes large enough to allow you to work comfortably. (For information about removing wall and floor coverings, see pages 114–124.)

Basically, tying into drainwaste, vent, and supply lines entails cutting a section out of each pipe and inserting a new fitting to join old and new pipe. The method you use to tie into the pipes varies with the pipe material.

Route new pipes. With the connections made, the new DWV and supply pipes are run to the new fixture location. Ideally, new drainpipes should be routed below the bathroom floor. They can be suspended from floor joists by pipe hangers, inserted in the space between parallel joists, or run through

notches or holes drilled in joists that are at right angles to the pipe (if allowed by code). If you have a finished basement or your bathroom is on the second floor, you'll need to cut into the ceiling to install pipes between or through joists, hide the pipes with a dropped ceiling, or box them in. (Remember that drainpipes must slope away from fixtures at a minimum slope of ¼ inch per foot.)

Supply pipes normally follow drainpipes, but for convenience they can be routed directly up through the wall or floor from main horizontal lines below. Supply pipes should run parallel to each other, at least 6 inches apart.

Build a wet wall. The main soil stack, and often a secondary stack, commonly hide inside an oversize house wall called a "wet wall."

Unlike an ordinary 2 by 4 stud wall (shown on page 84), a wet wall has a sole plate and a top plate built from 2 by 6 or 2 by 8 lumber. Additionally, the 2 by 4 studs are set in pairs, with flat sides facing out. This construction creates maximum space inside the wall for large DWV pipes (which often have an outer diameter greater than 3½ inches) and for the fittings which are wider yet.

You can also "fur out" an existing wall to hide added pipes—attach new 2 by 4s to the old ones, then add new wall coverings. Similarly, a new branch drain that can't run below the floor may be hidden by a raised section of floor.

Roughing-in fixtures

Following are general notes on roughing-in new fixtures that require tying into your present DWV and supply systems, or extending them. Note that fixtures may be required to have air chambers—dead-end pipes that minimize noisy water hammer.

Sink. A sink is comparatively easy to install. Common installations are back-to-back (requires little pipe), within a vanity cabinet (hides pipe runs), and side-by-side. A sink can often be wet vented if it's within the critical distance; otherwise it's back vented. Adding a sink has little impact on the drain's present efficiency (a sink rates low in fixture units).

Supply pipes required: Hot and cold stubouts with shutoff valves; transition fittings, if necessary; flexible tubing above shutoff valves (see "Sink faucets," page 108).

Toilet. The single most troublesome fixture to install, a toilet requires its own vent (2-inch minimum) and at least a 3-inch drain. If it's on a branch drain, a toilet can't be upstream from a sink or shower.

The closet bend and toilet floor flange must be roughed-in first; the floor flange must be positioned at the level of the eventual finished floor.

Supply pipes required: Cold water stubout with shutoff valve; flexible tubing above valve (see "Installing a toilet," page 112).

Shower stall and bathtub. Like sinks, bathtubs and showers rate low in fixture units. They're often positioned on branch drains and are usually wet-vented or back-vented; both enter the stack at floor level or below because of the below-floor trap. A shower's faucet body and shower head assembly are installed while the wall is open; tubs and showers may require support framing.

Supply pipes required: Hot and cold supply lines and a pipe to the shower head (see "Bathtub and shower faucets," page 109).

ROUGHING-IN FIXTURES

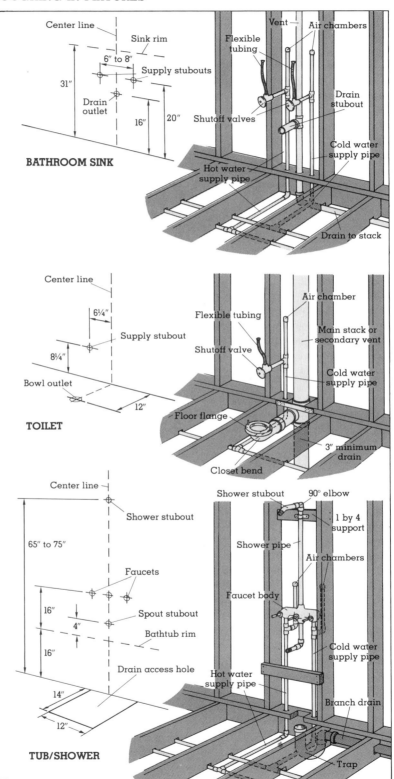

Representative roughing-in measurements. Plumbing components illustrated are a sink, toilet, and tub/shower. Use the measurements to help you plan; check local codes and specific fixture dimensions for exact roughing-in requirements.

Electrical basics

What may appear to be a hopelessly tangled maze of wires running through the walls, under the floors, and above the ceiling of your home is actually a well-organized system composed of several electrical circuits. In your bathroom, those circuits supply power to light fixtures, switches, fans, heaters, and electrical outlets.

This section briefly explains your home's electrical system and offers general information about basic electrical improvements so you can better understand the processes involved in making changes to your electrical system. Techniques for installing light fixtures appear on pages 94–95.

Before you do any work yourself, talk with your building department's electrical inspector about local codes, the National Electrical Code (NEC), and your area's requirements for permits and inspections.

Understanding your system

Today most homes have what's called "three-wire" service. The utility company connects three wires to your service entrance panel. Each of two hot wires supplies electricity at approximately 120 volts. A third wire—a neutral one—is maintained at zero volts. (Don't be misled, though; all three wires are live.)

Three-wire service provides both 120-volt and 240-volt capabilities. One hot wire and the neutral wire combine to provide 120 volts—primarily for lights and plug-in outlets. Two hot wires combine to provide 240 volts, often used for electric heaters.

Service entrance panel. This panel is the control center for your electrical system. Inside the panel, you'll usually find the main disconnect (main fuses or circuit breaker), the fuses or circuit breakers protecting each individual circuit, and the grounding connection for the entire system.

Simple circuitry. The word "circuit" means the course electric cur-

rent travels—in a continuous path from the service entrance panel or a separate subpanel, through one or more devices in your home that use electricity (such as light fixtures or appliances), and back to the panel. The devices are connected to the circuit by parallel wiring. With parallel wiring, a hot, a neutral, and a ground wire (for a 120-volt circuit) run continuously from one fixture box, outlet box, or switch box to another. Wires branch off to individual electrical devices from these continuous wires.

Circuit wires are housed together in a cable. Cable contains either one or two hot wires, a neutral wire, and a ground wire—each, except the ground wire, wrapped in its own insulation. (For the best connections, use only cable with all-copper wire.)

Individual wires are color-coded for easy identification. Hot wires are usually black or red, but may be any color other than white, gray, or green. Neutral wires are white or gray. Grounding wires are bare copper or green.

Occasionally, a white wire will be used as a hot wire; it should be taped or painted black near terminals and splices for easy identification.

Grounding. The NEC requires that every circuit have a ground wire. The ground wire provides an auxiliary path to ground for any short that might occur in a fixture or appliance. Also, according to the NEC, all bathroom outlets must be protected with ground fault circuit interrupters

(GFCI). These fast-acting circuit breakers cut off power within $\frac{1}{40}$ of a second if the current begins leaking anywhere along the circuit. They may be special circuit breakers, or they may be built into an outlet.

Extending a circuit

To extend an existing electrical circuit, you'll need a knack for making wire connections, and the patience to route new cable.

Before you start work, remember: NEVER WORK ON ANY LIVE CIRCUIT, FIXTURE, PLUG-IN OUTLET, OR SWITCH. Your life may depend on it. Turn off the circuit breaker or remove the fuse and make sure no one but you can turn the electricity back on.

The steps in extending a circuit are outlined below. Generally, you route new cable from box to box; you install new boxes where you want to add outlets, fixtures, or switches; and then you tap into a power source —an existing outlet, switch, or fixture box.

To install a new circuit, the work is much the same, except that you connect into a service panel or subpanel instead of into an existing outlet, switch, or fixture box.

Select a power source. A circuit can be tapped for power at almost any accessible outlet, switch, or fixture box of the appropriate voltage. (The exceptions are a switch box without a neutral wire and a fixture box at the end of a circuit.) The box you tap into must be large enough to hold new wires in addition to exist-

ROUTING CABLE TO OUTLETS

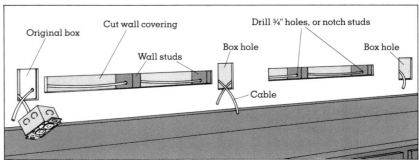

Original box · Cut wall covering · Wall studs · Drill ¾" holes, or notch studs · Box hole · Cable · Box hole

ing wires, and must have knockout holes through which you can run the new cable.

Select and locate new boxes. If wall or ceiling coverings have not yet been installed, choose an outlet or switch box you nail to studs or joists. If wall or ceiling coverings are already in place, choose cut-in boxes that don't have to be secured to studs or joists. Requirements regarding boxes for mounting ceiling fixtures are outlined on pages 94–95.

Unless codes prohibit the use of plastic, you can use either plastic or metal boxes. Metal boxes, though sturdier, must be grounded; plastic boxes cost less and need not be grounded, though the circuit must have a ground wire.

To find a suitable box location, first turn off power to all circuits that may be behind the wall or ceiling. Drill a small test hole and probe through it with a length of stiff insulated wire until you find an empty space.

Unless old boxes are at different levels, place new outlet boxes 12 to 18 inches above the floor, switch boxes or outlet boxes above a counter 44 inches above the floor. Never place boxes near a tub or shower.

If you're adding a new wall, you may be required by code to add an outlet every 12 feet, or one per wall regardless of the wall's length.

When you've determined the correct locations, trace the outline of each box on the wall or ceiling (omit protruding brackets). Then cut along the outlines.

Route and connect new cable. After the box holes are cut, run cable from the power source to each new box location (see illustration at left). (Wait until you have the new boxes wired and the outlets, switches, and fixtures connected before you make the actual hookup to the source.)

Where you have access from an unfinished basement, an unfloored attic, or a garage adjacent to the bathroom, it's easy to run cable either attached to the joists or studs

or through holes drilled in them.

Where walls and ceilings are covered on both sides, you'll have to fish cable through them, using electrician's fish tape (illustrated below) or a length of stiff wire with one end bent into a blunt, tight hook.

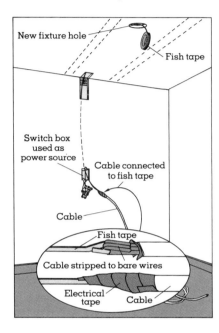

After routing new cable, secure the cable to each new box. Slip a cable connector onto the end of the cable and insert the cable and connector into a knockout in the box. Fasten the connector to the box, leaving 6 to 8 inches of cable sticking out for wiring connections. Then mount the box to the ceiling or wall and wire as described below.

Wire plug-in outlets. An outlet must have the same amperage and voltage rating as the circuit. If you have aluminum wiring, be sure to use the correct outlet; it will be identified by the letters CO-ALR. An outlet marked CU-AL should be used only with copper wire. If installing a GFCI outlet, follow the manufacturer's directions.

If you are adding a grounded outlet to a circuit that does not contain a grounding wire, you'll have to run a separate grounding wire from the new outlet to a nearby cold water pipe. (Check with your electrical inspector first.)

The drawing below shows how to wire a plug-in bathroom outlet with both halves live. The box is assumed to be metal; if you use a plastic box, there's no need to ground the box, but you'll have to attach a grounding wire to each outlet. Simply loop the end of the wire under the grounding screw. Connect the hot wire to the brass screw of the outlet, the neutral wire to the silver screw, and the ground wire to the green screw.

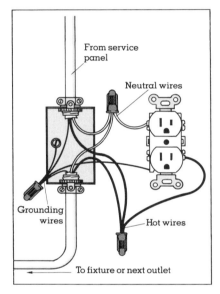

Wire single-pole switches. One single-pole switch may control one or more light fixtures, a heater, a ventilating fan, or several outlets.

Like outlets, the switch must have the same amperage and voltage rating as the circuit. If you have aluminum wiring, be sure to use a switch marked with the letters CO-ALR.

When wiring switches, remember that they are installed only on hot wires. The switches illustrated on page 94 have no grounding wires because the toggles on most home switches are made of shockproof plastic. If switches are housed in plastic boxes, the boxes do not need to be grounded. When installing a plastic switch box at the end of a circuit, secure the end of the grounding wire between the switch bracket and mounting screw. If the switch is in the middle of a circuit, just twist

...Electrical basics

WIRING SINGLE-POLE SWITCHES

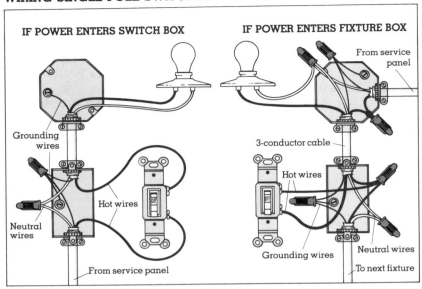

IF POWER ENTERS SWITCH BOX

Grounding wires

Neutral wires

Hot wires

From service panel

IF POWER ENTERS FIXTURE BOX

From service panel

3-conductor cable

Hot wires

Grounding wires

Neutral wires

To next fixture

Installing light fixtures

Most bathrooms need both general lighting and task lighting for specific areas. For a discussion of lighting choices, see pages 30 and 38.

Basically, to replace an existing light fixture with one of the same type, you disconnect the wires of the old fixture and hook up new wires. Adding a new fixture where there was none before is more complicated. You must first run new cable from a power source and install a fixture box and a switch.

Below are instructions for installing two types of light fixtures—surface-mounted and recessed.

Surface-mounted fixtures. Attach these fixtures directly to a wall or ceiling fixture box, or suspend ceiling fixtures from a fixture box by chains or cord. New fixtures usually come with their own mounting hardware, adaptable to any fixture box.

Sometimes, though, the weight of the new fixture or the wiring necessary for proper grounding requires that you replace the box before installing the fixture.

Electrical code requirements sometimes allow ceiling fixtures weighing less than 24 ounces to be mounted on cut-in boxes held in po-

the ends of the ground wires together and cover them with a wirenut.

Single-pole switches have two screw terminals of the same color (usually brass) for wire connections, and a definite right-side up. You should be able to read the words ON and OFF embossed on the toggle. It makes no difference which hot wire goes to which terminal. The cable can be run first either to the fixture or

to the switch—whichever is the more convenient route.

Wire into the power source. After you've wired new outlets and switches, you're ready to make the final connections. Connections to three types of boxes used as power sources are illustrated below. Wirenuts join and protect the stripped ends of spliced wires within the boxes.

WIRING INTO A POWER SOURCE

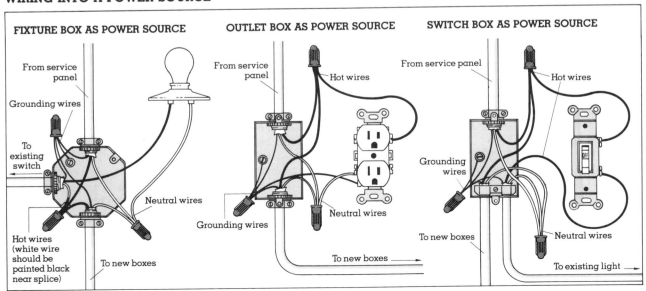

FIXTURE BOX AS POWER SOURCE

From service panel

Grounding wires

To existing switch

Hot wires (white wire should be painted black near splice)

To new boxes

Neutral wires

OUTLET BOX AS POWER SOURCE

From service panel

Hot wires

Grounding wires

Neutral wires

To new boxes

SWITCH BOX AS POWER SOURCE

From service panel

Hot wires

Grounding wires

To new boxes

Neutral wires

To existing light

sition by the ceiling material. For a more secure installation and for heavier fixtures, you must fasten the box to a framing member or a special bracket secured to the joists. Do not attach fixtures heavier than 6 pounds to the box with screws through the fixture's metal canopy; use the hardware supplied by the manufacturer or check with the electrical inspector.

The NEC requires that all incandescent and fluorescent fixtures with exposed metal parts be grounded. If the fixture box itself is grounded, the nipple or screws holding the fixture to the box will ground the fixture. (One exception: a cord or chain-hung fixture needs a grounding wire run from the socket to the box.) Most new fixtures are prewired with a grounding wire.

If the fixture box is not grounded, you'll probably have to extend a grounding wire from the box to the nearest cold water pipe (check first with your electrical inspector).

Install your new surface-mounted fixture as described below.

- **To replace an existing fixture with a new one,** first turn off the circuit. Remove the shade, if any, from the old fixture. Unscrew the canopy from the fixture box, and detach the mounting bar if there is one. Now make a sketch of how the wires are connected. If the wires are spliced with wirenuts, unscrew them and untwist the wires. If the wires are spliced and wrapped with electrician's tape, simply unwind the tape and untwist the wires. Match the wires of the new fixture to the old wires shown in your sketch, and splice with wirenuts. Secure the new fixture as recommended by the manufacturer, using any new hardware included. If you need to patch the wall or ceiling, see page 116.

- **To install a fixture in a new location,** you must route a new cable from a power source and install new fixture and switch boxes. New cable routed to the fixture box should include a grounding wire to be attached to the box's grounding

screw. If more than one cable enters the box (for example, a separate cable from the switch box), you'll need to attach the end of a short length of bare 12-gauge wire (a "jumper") to the grounding screw, and use a wirenut to splice its other end to the ends of the grounding wires in the cables. Once you've routed the new cable and grounded the fixture box, wire in the new fixture—black wire to black, white to white; cap all splices with wirenuts. Then mount the fixture with hardware supplied by the manufacturer.

Recessed ceiling fixtures. Incandescent recessed fixtures, or downlights, are installed in the ceiling. One type of fixture (shown at right) is prewired and grounded to a box mounted on a metal frame. Another type (below right) must be wired into a separate box already nailed to a joist.

Before installing either kind of fixture in a new location, you'll need to cut a hole in the ceiling between joists or remove tiles or panels from a suspended ceiling.

First, determine the proper location. Recessed fixtures need several inches of clearance above the finished ceiling. They're most easily installed below an unfinished attic or crawlspace. Because of the heat generated by recessed fixtures, you must also allow adequate air flow around the fixture. In addition, remove insulation within 3 inches of the fixture, and make sure that no combustible materials are within ½ inch (with the exception of joists or special 2 by 4 blocking used for supporting larger fixtures).

When you've determined the location, trace the outline of the fixture housing or frame on the ceiling with a pencil. Use a keyhole saw or saber saw to cut a neat hole.

To install a fixture prewired to its box, first slip the metal frame and box through the hole cut in the ceiling and then clip it to the ceiling's edge. Snap the fixture housing into its socket and secure it to the frame with the swivel clips.

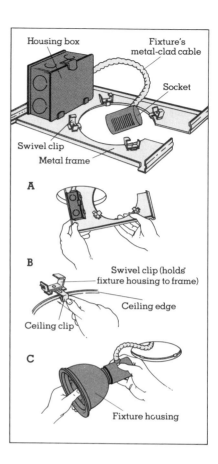

To install a fixture without a box, nail a box to a joist and wire it. Connect the fixture's metal-clad wires and socket to the wires in the box, and install a cover. Plug the socket into the fixture housing and fasten the housing to the ceiling, using the clips supplied with the light.

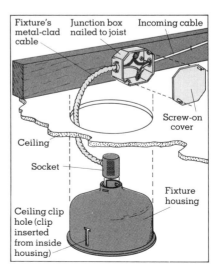

CLIMATE CONTROL: HEATING & VENTILATION

Certain elements of your bathroom's climate—steam, excess heat, early morning chill—can be annoying and unpleasant. When you remodel, consider adding an exhaust fan to freshen the air and draw out destructive moisture, and a heater to warm you on cool days. Installing these climate controllers is within the grasp of most do-it-yourselfers. On these pages, we explore some of your heating and ventilating options.

Heating the bathroom

Nothing spoils the soothing effects of a long, hot soak or shower faster than stepping out into a cool bathroom. A small heater in the wall or ceiling may be just what you need to stay warm while toweling off.

Bathroom heaters warm rooms by two methods—convection (usually boosted by a small fan) and radiation. Convection heaters warm the air in a room; the air, in turn, transfers the heat to surfaces and objects that it contacts. Radiant heaters emit infrared or electromagnetic waves that warm objects and surfaces they hit, without warming the intervening air.

You can buy both convection and radiant electric heaters for mounting in the wall or ceiling. Gas models are usually wall-mounted convection heaters.

Electric heaters. Because electric heaters are easy to install and clean to operate, they're the most popular choice for heating bathrooms. In addition to the standard wall and ceiling-mounted units, you'll find heaters combined with exhaust fans, lights, or both (see illustrations below). Options include thermostats, timer switches, and safety cutoffs.

Wall or ceiling-mounted convection heaters usually have an electrically heated resistance coil and a small fan to move the heated air.

Radiant heaters using infrared light bulbs may be surface-mounted on the ceiling or recessed between the joists. Radiant heating panels are generally flush-mounted on a wall or ceiling.

If you're planning to replace the wallboard on a wall or ceiling, you might consider using gypsum wallboard panels with electric resistance wires embedded in them. Your whole ceiling or wall will become a radiant heating panel.

If you're installing a suspended ceiling, you might want to replace some of the ceiling panels with radiant heating panels.

Gas heaters. You'll find heaters available for either propane or natural gas. Though most are convection heaters, there is one radiant type—a catalytic heater. Regardless of how they heat, all gas models require a gas supply line and must be vented to the outside.

Gas heaters that can be recessed into a wall between two studs are available in a variety of styles and sizes. Options include electric ignition and wall-mounted thermostats.

Installation tips. Choose the location of your heater carefully. Of course you'll want to place it where someone getting out of the tub or shower will benefit from it (this is particularly true of radiant heaters, which heat objects directly). But don't locate the heater where someone will bump against its hot surfaces, or where it might char or ignite curtains or towels.

Since gas heaters require a vent to the outside, you'll probably want to place the heater on an outside wall. Otherwise you'll have to run the vent through the attic or crawlspace and out through the roof.

ELECTRIC HEATERS

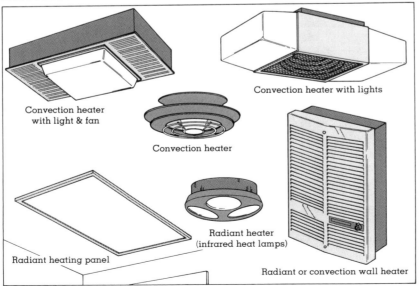

Convection heater with light & fan

Convection heater with lights

Convection heater

Radiant heating panel

Radiant heater (infrared heat lamps)

Radiant or convection wall heater

Ventilating the bathroom

Most building codes require that bathrooms have either natural or forced ventilation. The bathroom is a major source of destructive moisture as well as hazardous pollutants, unpleasant odors, and excess heat.

Obviously, forced ventilation is required in windowless bathrooms; in fact, some codes specify that the exhaust fan must be on the same switch as the lights. But even if you have natural ventilation, you may want to consider forced ventilation as well. An exhaust fan can exchange the air in a bathroom much faster than a wide-open window can; and in bad weather, it can keep the elements out and still remove stale air.

Choosing an exhaust fan.
You can buy fans to mount in the wall or in the ceiling. Some models are combined with a light or a heater (see illustrations above right) or both.

It's important that your exhaust fan have adequate capacity. The Home Ventilating Institute (HVI) recommends that the fan be capable of exchanging the air at least eight times every hour. To determine the required fan capacity in cubic feet per minute (CFM) for a bathroom with an 8-foot ceiling, multiply the room's length and width in feet by 1.1. For example, if your bathroom is 6 by 9 feet, you would calculate the required fan capacity as follows:

$$6 \times 9 \times 1.1 = 59.4 \, CFM$$

Rounding off, you would need fan capacity of at least 60 CFM. If your fan must exhaust through a long duct or several elbows, you'll need greater capacity to overcome the increased resistance. Follow the dealer's or manufacturer's recommendations.

Most fans also have a noise rating measured in sones; the lower the number, the quieter the fan.

Installation tips.
Ideally, the fan should be mounted as close to the shower or tub as possible. It should also be as far away as possible from

EXHAUST FANS

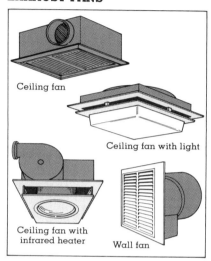

Ceiling fan

Ceiling fan with light

Ceiling fan with infrared heater

Wall fan

the source of replacement air (the door, for instance). In addition, you'll want the exhaust duct to be as short and as straight as possible. If you have trouble finding a location that meets all three requirements, you may want to consult a professional.

THREE WAYS TO DUCT EXHAUST FANS

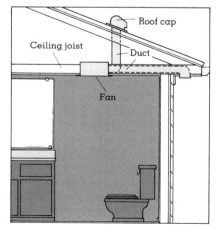

Roof cap

Ceiling joist

Duct

Fan

Ceiling fan ventilates through duct either to roof cap on roof or to grill in soffit under the eave.

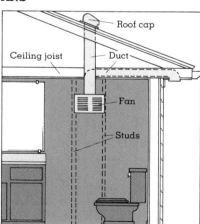

Roof cap

Ceiling joist

Duct

Fan

Studs

Wall fan on inside wall also ventilates through duct to cap on roof or to grill in soffit under the eave.

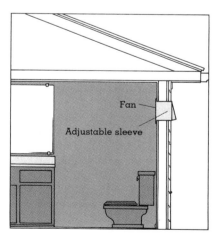

Fan

Adjustable sleeve

Wall fan on outside wall, installed between wall studs, ventilates through wall directly to outside.

Sinks

Replacing the bathroom sink (also known as a lavatory or basin) is one of the quickest ways to give your bathroom a new look without getting involved in a complex and expensive remodeling project.

This section will show you how to remove and install the four basic types of sinks: integral sink and countertop, pedestal, wall-hung, and deck-mount. For more information on these sink models and materials, see page 32.

If you're planning to add a sink or to move one, you may want to consult a professional about extending supply, drain, and vent lines (see pages 88–91). But to replace a sink, extensive experience with plumbing isn't a requirement.

REMOVING A SINK

Unless you'll be installing a new floor covering, be sure to protect the bathroom floor with a piece of plywood before you begin work. You'll also want a bucket and a supply of rags or sponges nearby to soak up excess water.

To loosen corroded plumbing connections, douse them with penetrating oil an hour before you start.

Disconnecting the plumbing

If the sink faucet is mounted on the countertop and you don't plan to replace the faucet, it isn't necessary to disconnect the water supply lines. If the faucet is connected to the sink, you do need to disconnect the supply lines.

Be sure to turn off the water at the sink shutoff valves or at the main valve before doing any work. Disconnect the supply lines at the shutoff valves, placing a bucket underneath them to catch any water, and open the faucets so the lines can drain.

If your sink isn't equipped with shutoff valves, disconnect the supply lines at the faucet inlet shanks, as explained on page 108—and plan on adding shutoff valves before you connect the plumbing to the new sink

(have a professional plumber do the work for you).

Next, move the bucket underneath the trap. If the trap has a cleanout plug, remove it to drain the water, then loosen the slip nuts and remove the trap. If there is no cleanout plug, remove the trap and dump the water into the bucket.

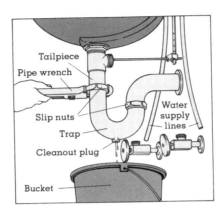

Disconnect the pop-up drain assembly by loosening the clevis screw and removing the spring clip that connects the stopper and pivot rod to the pop-up rod on the faucet (see "Removing a sink faucet," page 108).

The tailpiece, drain body, and sink flange, as well as the faucet, will now come out with the sink. If you plan to reuse the old faucet, remove it carefully from the sink and set aside.

Removing an integral sink & countertop

An integral sink is molded as part of the countertop, and the unit is secured to the top of a vanity cabinet. Look underneath for any metal clips or wooden braces securing the unit, and remove them. Then lift off the whole unit.

If you can't remove the unit easily, insert the end of a small prybar in the joint between the countertop and vanity cabinet at a back corner. Carefully lift up the prybar to break the sealing material between the countertop and the vanity. If the joint is too narrow to accept the end of a prybar, cut through the sealing ma-

terial with a hot putty knife, then pry or lift up the countertop.

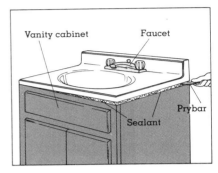

Removing a pedestal sink

Most pedestal sinks are made of two pieces—the sink and the pedestal or base. Look in the opening at the rear of the pedestal to locate a nut or bolt holding the sink down. If you find one, remove it. Lift off the sink and set it aside.

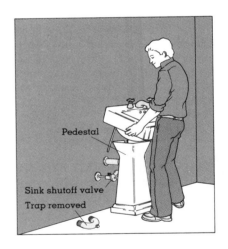

The pedestal is usually bolted to the floor. You may find the bolts on the base, or on the inside of the pedestal (see illustration above right). Undo the bolts and remove the pedestal. If you can't move it after removing the bolts, rock it back and forth, and then lift it out. If the pedestal is recessed into a ceramic tile floor, you may have to remove the surrounding floor tiles with a cold chisel and soft-headed steel hammer. Rock the pedestal back and forth to break any remaining seal with the floor. Lift the pedestal up and set it aside.

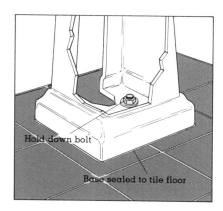

Removing a wall-hung sink

To remove a wall-hung sink, first unscrew the legs, if any, that support the front of the sink. Check underneath for any bolts securing the sink to the mounting bracket on the wall (see illustration below), and remove them. Then lift the sink straight up and off the mounting bracket.

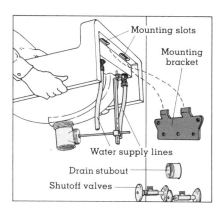

Removing a deck-mount sink

There are three basic types of deck-mount sinks used in vanity countertops: self-rimming or rimless sinks, flush-mount sinks, and unrimmed or recessed sinks. All may be secured to the countertop with lugs or clamps that must be unscrewed before you remove the sink.

Self-rimming or rimless sinks.
These have a molded flange that sits on the countertop. Once you have removed any lugs or clamps from underneath, just use a hot putty knife or other knife to cut through the

sealing material between sink and countertop; then pry up the sink to break the seal and lift it out.

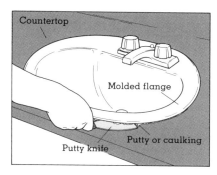

Flush-mount sinks. Have a helper support the sink while you undo the lugs or clamps that secure the sink's metal rim to the countertop. (If you're working alone, you can support the sink with a 2 by 4 and a wood block tied together through the drain; see illustration below). After you remove the lugs or clamps, cut through the sealing material between the rim and the countertop with a hot putty knife or other knife. Pry up the rim to free the sink; then lift straight up.

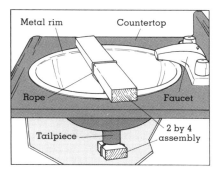

Unrimmed or recessed sinks.
An unrimmed or recessed sink is secured to the underside of the countertop. The easiest way to remove the sink is to first take off the countertop. Check underneath for any brackets and remove them. Then insert a prybar into the joint between the countertop and the vanity cabinet near a rear corner, and pry up. Turn the countertop bottom side up and rest it on a padded surface. Undo the lugs or clamps securing the sink, and lift it off the countertop.

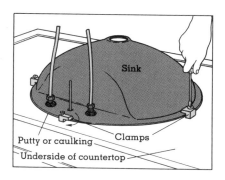

When the countertop is tiled, the flange usually rests on top of the plywood base for the tile. Look underneath; if you don't see any clips or brackets, you'll have to remove the tile surrounding the edge of the sink. With a soft-headed steel hammer and cold chisel, remove enough tile so that you can lift the sink from the countertop. (Be sure to protect your eyes with goggles.) If you can't find matching replacement tile and need to reuse the old tiles, remove them carefully to avoid breaking them.

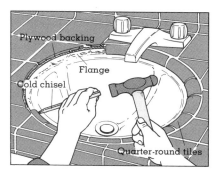

INSTALLING A SINK

If you're installing a sink at a new location instead of replacing an existing one, you'll need to extend the water, drain, and vent pipes (see pages 88–91).

If you'd like your sink to be higher than standard, you can raise the vanity of an integral or deck-mount sink by building a base under it. If you're installing a wall-hung sink, simply mount the bracket higher. You can't adjust the height of a pedestal sink, but you may be able to buy a taller model.

(Continued on next page)

. . . Sinks

INSTALLING A SINK FAUCET

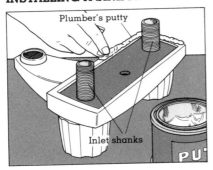

Apply putty to bottom edge of the faucet if there is no rubber gasket to seal it to sink's surface.

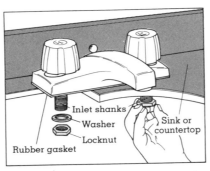

Set the faucet in place, insert inlet shanks through sink holes, and press faucet onto sink. Install washers and locknuts.

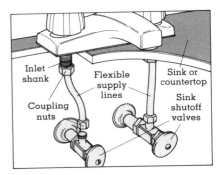

Attach flexible supply lines to the sink shutoff valves, using coupling nuts on each end.

Before installing the sink, you'll need to install the faucet and the sink flange.

Installing the faucet & sink flange

Whether the faucet is to be mounted on the countertop or on the sink itself, you'll find it easier to install the faucet before you set the sink in place. The main steps are illustrated above. First make sure that the mounting surface is clean. If your faucet came with a rubber gasket, place it on the bottom of the faucet. For a faucet without a gasket, put a bead of plumber's putty around the bottom edge of the faucet.

Set the faucet in position, and press it down onto the sink or countertop surface. Assemble the washers and locknuts on the inlet shanks, and then tighten the nuts. Remove excess putty from around the faucet. Connect the supply lines to the inlet shanks and tighten the coupling nuts. For more information on installing faucets, see pages 108–109.

Now install the sink flange and drain. To attach the flange, run a bead of plumber's putty around the drain hole of the sink. Press the flange into the puttied hole. Put the locknut, metal washer, and flat rubber washer on the drain body in that order. Insert the threaded end of the drain body into the bottom of the sink and screw it onto the flange. Then tighten the locknut until it is snug (do not overtighten).

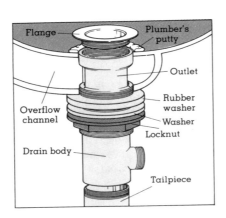

Installing an integral sink & countertop

Cover the top edges of the vanity cabinet with a sealant recommended by the manufacturer. Place the countertop unit on the cabinet flush with the back edge. Make sure the overhang—if any—is equal on the left and right. Press along the countertop edges to complete the seal, and check around the perimeter, removing any excess sealant.

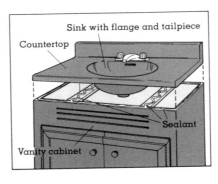

If your unit came with mounting brackets, use them to secure the countertop to the vanity. Seal the joint between the countertop and the wall with caulking compound.

Installing a pedestal sink

First position the pedestal on the floor, with the sink resting on top. Center the pedestal in front of the drain stubout; then set the sink aside. Use the holes in the base to mark the locations of the hold-down bolts.

Set the pedestal and sink to one side and drill pilot holes for the bolts. Put a bead of plumber's putty or caulking compound around the bottom edge of the pedestal; then bolt it in place.

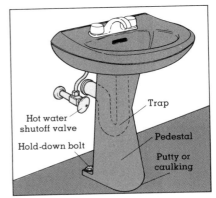

Position the sink on top of the pedestal and, if required by the manufacturer, bolt the two together as directed.

Installing a wall-hung sink

For new installations, you'll need to remove the wall coverings and wallboard. Notch two studs directly behind the sink's proposed location, and nail or screw a 1 by 6 or 1 by 8 mounting board to the studs; then re-cover the wall.

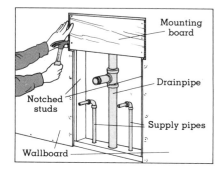

Before you attach the mounting bracket to the wall mounting board, check to see that it fits the sink. Refer to the manufacturer's instructions to properly position the bracket. Generally, you center the bracket over the drainpipe, then level it at the desired height from the floor. Fasten the bracket to the mounting board with woodscrews, making sure that it's level. Then carefully lower the sink onto the mounting bracket.

Because the mounting bracket can bend or break under the weight of a large wall-hung sink, the manufacturer may recommend that adjustable legs be inserted into the holes under the front corners of the sink. Screw the legs down until the sink is level; be sure to keep the legs plumb.

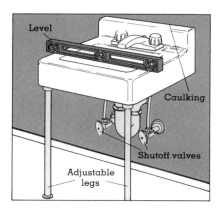

Seal the joint between the back of the sink and the wall with caulking compound.

Installing a deck-mount sink

If your countertop doesn't have a hole for the sink, you'll need to cut one. For a self-rimming or an un-rimmed sink, mark the hole, using the templates supplied with the sink. If you didn't receive a template, cut one from paper; it should fit loosely around the outside of the sink bowl where the bowl meets the flange.

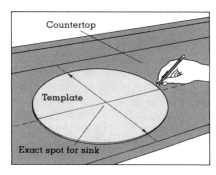

For a flush-mount sink, trace the outside edge of the sink's metal framing rim directly onto the spot where the sink will sit in the countertop.

After you mark the location of the cutout, drill a starting hole, then use a saber saw to cut the opening.

Install your deck-mount sink as described below.

Self-rimming or rimless sinks.
First, run a bead of caulking compound or plumber's putty around the underside of the flange. Set the sink on the countertop and press it down until the putty oozes out. Install any lugs or clamps according to the manufacturer's instructions. Remove excess putty.

Flush-mount sinks.
Apply a bead of caulking compound or plumber's putty around the sink lip. Fasten the metal framing rim around the lip, following the manufacturer's directions. Next, apply a bead of caulking compound or plumber's putty

around the top edge of the countertop sink opening, and set the sink and rim in place. Secure the sink and rim to the underside of the countertop with the lugs or clamps provided. Wipe off excess putty.

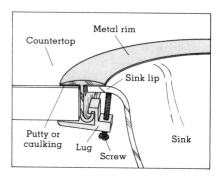

Unrimmed or recessed sinks.
Turn the countertop upside down and apply caulking compound or plumber's putty on the underside, around the edge of the sink opening. Set the sink in place, checking from the other side to be sure it is centered in the opening. Anchor the sink as recommended by the manufacturer. If you're finishing the countertop with ceramic tile, you can mount the sink under the plywood countertop base as illustrated on page 99.

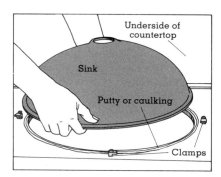

Connecting the plumbing

Once the sink is installed, you can connect the water supply lines to the shutoff valves and tighten the coupling nuts. Then connect the trap to the drainpipe and tailpiece, and tighten the slip nuts (see illustration, page 98). Connect the pop-up stopper to the faucet pop-up rod. Turn on the water at the shutoff valves or main shutoff and check for leaks.

Bathtubs

Installing or replacing a bathtub can be a complicated job—one that takes careful planning. But a gleaming new tub in your bathroom is well worth the effort.

Your tub choices range from porcelain-enameled cast iron or steel to lightweight fiberglass-reinforced plastic. The waterproof wall covering around a tub can be tile or panels of fiberglass-reinforced plastic (often called a surround).

If you're building a new bathroom, you can create an entire bath area with a tub and surround manufactured as a one-piece unit. These units are not recommended for remodeling projects, though, since they are usually too large to fit through a door and must be moved in before the bathroom walls are framed. For remodeling, your best choice is a tub with separate wall panels or tiles.

Before you install a tub in a new location, check local building codes for support requirements; a bathtub filled with water is extremely heavy and needs plenty of support. You should also check the plumbing code requirements for extending the water supply and drain-waste and vent systems (see page 89). Consider getting professional help to build the framing and to rough-in plumbing for a new installation.

In this section, you'll find general directions for removing and installing bathtubs and wall coverings. For detailed product information, see page 35.

REMOVING A BATHTUB

There are three main steps to this job: disconnecting the appropriate plumbing, removing part or all of the wall covering, and removing the tub itself.

Disconnecting the plumbing

Generally it's not necessary to turn off the water unless you're replacing the faucet body. If you do need to turn off the water, do so at the fixture shutoff valves (if you can reach them through an access door in an adjoining room or hallway) or at the main shutoff valve. Open the faucets to drain the pipes.

Next, remove the fittings—spout, faucet parts, shower head, and diverter handle (see illustration below). The stubouts (short lengths of pipe) and the valve stems will remain protruding from the wall.

To remove the tub, you'll have to unscrew and remove the overflow cover and drain lever. By pulling out this fitting, you'll also remove the bathtub drain assembly if it's a trip-lever type.

If you have a pop-up stopper, pull it out with the rocker linkage after removing the overflow cover (see illustration below).

To disconnect the remaining pipes, you'll need to work through an access door, through a hole you've cut in the wall, or from the basement

or crawlspace below. Using a pipe wrench, loosen the slip nuts on the trap and remove it; then disconnect and remove the overflow pipe (see illustration below).

Removing the wall covering

Most bathtubs are recessed; that is; they are surrounded by walls on three sides. Depending on whether you want to replace the tub only, or the tub and the wall covering, you'll need to remove all or part of the surrounding tiles or panels. Before doing this, remove any fittings, such as the shower head, that are in the way (if you haven't yet done so).

Tile. If there are wall or floor tiles along the edge of the tub, free the tub by chipping out approximately 4 inches to the nearest grout joint (see illustration above right). On the walls, remove the plaster or gypsum wallboard backing at the same time, so that several inches of the wall studs are exposed. Use a cold chisel and soft-headed steel hammer to remove the tile, and be sure to protect your eyes from fragments by wearing goggles.

If you're removing a recessed tub, you must also remove enough tile (and other obstructions) from the floor and walls to be able to slide the tub out of its recess.

Fiberglass panels. Take out the wall panels by first removing the

DISCONNECTING THE PLUMBING

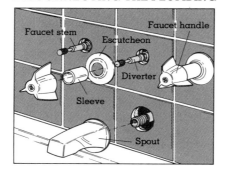

Remove faucet and diverter parts and spout, leaving stubout for spout and faucet and diverter stems.

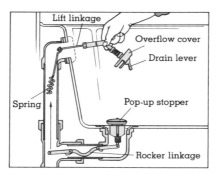

Unscrew overflow cover, then pull out drain assembly—first the overflow cover and lift linkage, then the pop-up stopper.

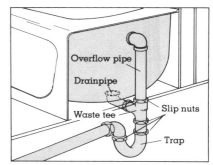

Loosen slip nuts and remove trap from underneath tub; then disconnect and remove overflow pipe.

REMOVING WALL COVERINGS

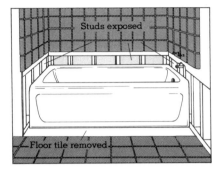

For tile walls, chip away a 4-inch strip of tile and backing from walls; remove an equivalent strip from a tile floor.

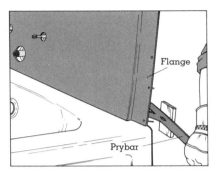

For fiberglass panels, pry panel flange and pull panel and any backing off the wall studs.

gypsum wallboard or molding from the panel flanges. With a prybar, pry the panels, along with any backing, off the studs. Once the end panels are removed, you can take out the back panel, leaving the exposed wall studs (see illustration above).

Removing the tub

The tub's bulk will make this one of your biggest jobs. To get the tub out, you may first have to remove the bathroom door or even cut a hole in the wall opposite the tub plumbing. Plan exactly how you'll route the tub through and out of the house. You'll need helpers to move it, especially if it's a heavy steel or cast-iron fixture.

Steel or cast-iron tubs. Locate and remove from the wall studs any nails or screws at the top of the tub's flange (lip) that may be holding the tub in place. With at least one helper (probably three for a cast-iron tub), lift up the tub with a prybar and slide two or three soaped wooden runners under it (see illustration at right). Then slide the tub out of the recess.

Fiberglass tubs. To remove a fiberglass or plastic tub, pull out all nails or screws driven into the wall studs through the flange. Reach between the studs and grasp the tub under the flange (see illustration far right); with the aid of a helper, if necessary, pull the tub up off its supports and out of the recess.

INSTALLING A BATHTUB

If you're replacing an old tub with a new one, carefully inspect the subfloor where the tub will be installed for level and for moisture damage, and make any necessary repairs or adjustments.

If you're installing a tub in a new location, you'll do the framing and rough-in the plumbing first (see "Structural basics," pages 83–86, and "Plumbing basics," pages 88–91).

Setting, leveling & securing the tub

This is the most crucial part of the installation process. A tub must be correctly supported and carefully secured in a level position so that it will drain properly and all plumbing connections can be made easily.

MOVING THE TUB

To move a steel or cast-iron tub, slide it across floor on soaped wooden runners. You'll need several helpers .

Steel or cast-iron tubs. These heavy tubs require either vertical or horizontal wood supports (see "Four ways to support a tub" on the following page). Horizontal supports are 1 by 4s or 2 by 4s, nailed across the wall studs so that the tub's flange rests on them. Vertical supports are 2 by 4s nailed to each stud. Position the supports so that the tub will be level both from end to end and from back to front.

If your tub is steel, you can attach prefabricated metal hangers to the studs with woodscrews to support the tub.

When you've attached the appropriate supports, slide your new tub along soaped wooden runners into position (see illustration below). With the aid of several helpers, lift it so that the flanges rest on the supports. Check the tub at both ends to see that it's level. If not, insert shims between the tub and wall supports or floor to level it. To prevent the tub from slipping, anchor it by driving nails or screws into the studs tight against the top of the flange.

Fiberglass tubs. If necessary, temporarily remove any protruding stubouts. Then, with a helper, set the tub on wood supports, tight against the rear studs.

Once the tub is in position, check on top for level at both ends, shimming where needed, as for steel and cast-iron models. Drill holes in the tub flange and carefully nail or screw through the holes into the studs.

(Continued on next page)

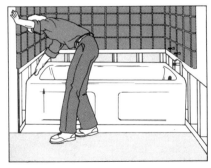

To move a fiberglass tub, grasp it under back of the flange and lift it up and out. A helper will make the job easier.

... Bathtubs

Connecting the plumbing

Once the tub is secured in position, reconnect the overflow pipe, trap, and drain assembly. (Be careful not to overtighten the nuts and crack the tub's surface.) Make sure you connect the overflow pipe with the tub drainpipe on the side of the trap nearest the bathtub, not on the far side.

Next, install the faucet and diverter parts, spout, and shower head. If you plan to install a new wall covering (see below), reconnect these fittings afterwards.

Installing the wall covering

Before patching or re-covering the walls with either tile or panels, turn on the water and check the drain and supply pipes for leaks.

If you plan to patch or install a tiled wall, see pages 114–121. Use water-resistant gypsum wallboard as backing.

To install new fiberglass panels, cover any exposed studs with water-resistant gypsum wallboard (cut to accommodate the plumbing) according to manufacturer's directions. Then follow the procedure outlined below.

Drill pipe holes. To install a panel over pipe stubouts and faucet and

FOUR WAYS TO SUPPORT A TUB

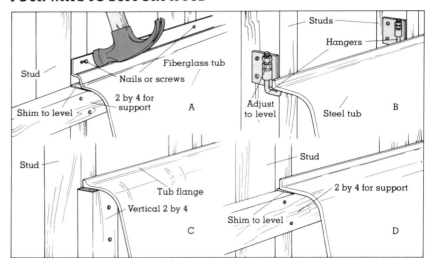

Support a new tub in one of these ways: nail or screw fiberglass tub flange to studs (A); support steel tub with metal hangers (B); nail vertical 2 by 4s to studs to support metal tubs (C); nail horizontal 2 by 4s to support metal tubs (D).

diverter stems, you'll need to mark and drill it accurately (see illustration below). Measure and mark the panel by holding it up against the stubouts and stems. Drill slightly oversized holes in the panel with a spade bit, backing the panel with a wood plank to prevent splintering.

Set panels. Apply mastic in S-patterns to the backs of the panels (see illustration below), and press

the panels in place around the top of the tub, according to manufacturer's directions. If panels are to be nailed or screwed to the studs, predrill all nail holes.

Finish and seal panels. Seal all gaps between the wall covering and the stubouts and stems with silicone caulk. Finally, re-attach the faucet and diverter parts, spout, and shower head.

INSTALLING PANELS AROUND A TUB

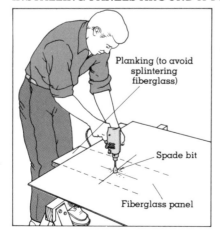

After carefully marking one panel to fit over the stubouts and faucet and diverter stems, drill holes in it with a spade bit.

Apply mastic to panel in S-patterns while panel rests on planks laid across a pair of sawhorses.

Press panel into place on the wall, fitting it over stubouts and faucet and diverter stems.

Showers

From elegant ceramic tile to easy-to-install fiberglass or plastic panels, your choices are many when it comes to replacing or adding a shower in your home. And if you're installing a completely new bathroom, you can also choose a molded one-piece shower enclosure. (These are not recommended for remodeling projects because they won't fit through most bathroom doors.)

In this section you'll find instructions for removing all types of showers (including the older metal units) and for installing tile and fiberglass-reinforced or plastic-paneled showers. For more details on various models, see page 34.

REMOVING A SHOWER

Most showers consist of three walls with waterproof wall covering, such as tile or panels, and a separate base, mounted in a wood frame. Removing a shower is a three-step procedure: disconnecting the plumbing, removing the wall covering, and removing the base. If the shower is a one-piece unit, you'll also have to cut a hole in a wall to get it out, unless you cut the unit into pieces.

If you're changing the location of a shower or permanently removing it, you'll probably want to dismantle the wood frame and remove the plumbing.

Disconnecting the plumbing

First remove the shower door or the rod and curtain. Then turn off the water supply at the fixture shutoff valves (sometimes accessible through an access door in an adjoining hallway or closet) or at the main shutoff valve. Open the faucets to drain the pipes. Then sponge the shower base dry.

Remove the faucet handles and other trim parts, leaving the faucet stems. Then remove the shower head with a pipe wrench tapewrapped to avoid scarring the fixture (see illustration above).

DISCONNECTING SHOWER PLUMBING

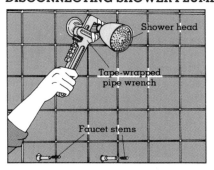

Use pipe wrench wrapped with tape to remove shower head. (Faucet parts have already been removed.)

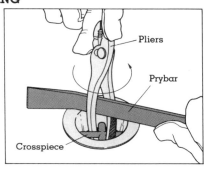

After removing drain cover, use pliers and prybar to unscrew crosspiece from drain.

Unscrew and pry up the drain cover, and with a pair of pliers and a small prybar, unscrew the crosspiece (see illustration). If you're removing a one-piece shower enclosure, you'll also have to disconnect the drainpipe and remove protruding faucet stems and fittings that might get in the way when you tip the unit to pull it out. Finally, plug the drain opening with a rag to prevent debris from falling into it.

Removing the wall covering

The removal procedure you'll follow depends on whether you have a tiled

shower, walls covered with fiberglass panels, or an older metal shower.

After you've removed the wall covering, check for moisture damage to the frame and to any soundproofing insulation secured across the inside of the frame. Repair or replace if necessary.

Tile. Ceramic tile is the most difficult wall covering to remove. If the existing tile is clean, smooth, and securely attached, you can avoid removing it by using it as a backing for a new tile surface. If you must remove it, proceed with caution and wear goggles while you work.

(Continued on next page)

REMOVING SHOWER WALLS

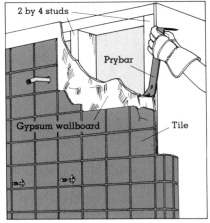

For tile walls, chip and pry off tile and wallboard backing to expose entire frame of shower.

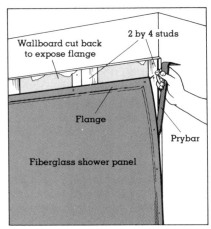

For panel walls, remove any wallboard or molding covering panel flanges; then pry panels off frame.

. . . Showers

To remove tile set in mortar, you must break up the tile, mortar, and any backing with a sledge hammer. Remove it down to the wood frame, being careful not to hit and damage the wall studs. You may want to hire a tile professional for this part of the project.

If the tile is set on wallboard with adhesive, use a cold chisel and soft-headed steel hammer to chip away small sections of tile and backing. Then insert a prybar and pry off large sections of tile and backing until the entire frame is exposed (see illustration, page 105).

Fiberglass panels. First remove any molding or wallboard covering the panel flanges. Then pry panels, along with any backing and nails, off the wood frame (see illustration, page 105). If you're removing a one-piece enclosure, you may have to cut it apart to get it out (a saber saw with a plastic-cutting blade will do the job quickly).

Metal showers. Remove metal shower walls by unscrewing them at the edges and then at the front and back corners. These screws hold the shower walls to each other and sometimes to a wood frame. If the screws are rusted, cut the screw heads off with a hacksaw or cold chisel; then separate the walls with a hard pull.

Removing the base

The base may be tile on a mortar bed, or it may be a fiberglass unit. Tile is difficult to remove because it's laid in mortar; fiberglass bases are simply pried out.

After you've removed the base, inspect the subfloor and framing for moisture damage, and repair where necessary.

Tile on mortar. As with tile walls, check first to see if you can lay the new tile over the old. If not, use a sledge hammer to break up and remove all tile and mortar down to the subfloor. You may be able to pry up one side of the base and slip a

wedge under it to make it easier to break up. Wear goggles to protect your eyes from tile or mortar fragments.

Fiberglass. Remove all nails or screws from the flange around the top of the base. Pry the base off the floor with a prybar; lift it out.

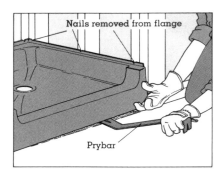

Nails removed from flange

Prybar

INSTALLING A SHOWER

When you replace an old shower, the plumbing—and probably the wood frame—will already be in place.

If you're putting a shower in a new location, you must first frame the shower walls using 2 by 4s (see "Structural Basics," pages 83–86). Make accurate measurements (follow manufacturer's directions to frame a fiberglass shower); keep framing square and plumb. Once the frame is complete, you'll also need to rough-in supply and drain lines, and install the faucet and the pipe for the shower head (see pages 88–91 and 110).

Now you're ready to install the shower—first the base, then the walls.

Installing the base

Installing a watertight tiled base on a mortar bed is a highly complicated project not recommended for beginners. If you want this type of base in either a tile or panel shower, consider having a professional build it.

To install a fiberglass or plastic base, position it over the drain outlet. Connect the base to the drain by screwing in the crosspiece (see il-

lustration, page 105), and cover the opening with rags to keep debris from falling in. Follow the manufacturer's directions to secure the base to the frame. Later, remove the rags and attach the drain cover with screws.

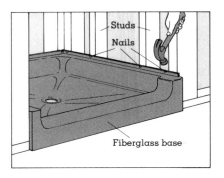

Studs

Nails

Fiberglass base

Installing the wall covering

Once the base is secured, you're ready to cover the shower's side and back walls with tile or panels.

Tile. Like a tile base, tile walls can be tricky to install. If you want tile on a mortar bed but aren't experienced at tiling, you may want to have a tile contractor install it. If you want tile backed with water-resistant gypsum wallboard, you may decide to do it yourself.

First, prepare the backing. Cut holes in the wallboard for the shower head stubout and faucet stems; then nail the wallboard to the frame (see illustration above right).

Plan the layout of your tile by marking horizontal and vertical working lines on the shower wall (see illustrations above right). Using thin-set adhesive, tile the back wall. Then move on to the sides, cutting tiles to fit around the shower stubout and faucet stems.

Set ceramic tile accessories. Allow the tile to set (for the required time, consult the adhesive manufacturer's instructions) before grouting all the joints between the tiles. When the grout has set, you can seal it. For more information on establishing working lines, setting tile, and grouting joints, turn to pages 119–121; or ask your tile dealer.

INSTALLING TILE ON SHOWER WALLS

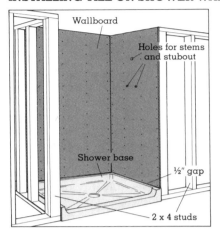

To attach wallboard to a wood shower frame, nail along the length of the 2 by 4 studs.

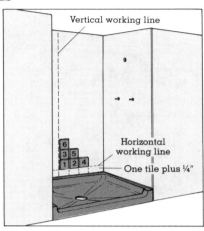

Mark working lines, both horizontal and vertical, then set tile on shower walls in a pyramid pattern.

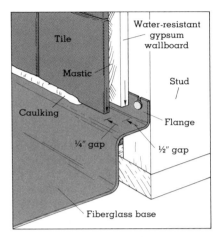

Water-resistant wallboard is positioned to leave ½-inch gap above base; leave ¼-inch gap for caulking tile.

Fiberglass panels. Shower panels of fiberglass usually come with manufacturer's directions for installation. Some require no backing (except perhaps soundproofing insulation); others require separate water-resistant wallboard backing.

For both types of panels, measure and mark on one panel the locations of the shower head stubout and faucet stems. Lay the marked panel across two sawhorses, and with a spade bit, drill slightly oversized holes for your fittings. Support the panels with wood planks so you don't splinter them as you drill (see

illustration below).

If the base of your shower has channels on the outside edges for sealant, clean out any debris from them. Then fill the groove at the back with the sealant recommended by the manufacturer (see illustration below). Also apply adhesive to the reverse side of the back panel according to manufacturer's directions.

Install the back panel by fitting it into the groove on the base, then pressing it against the frame to make a complete seal. Next, fill the other grooves on the base with seal-

ant and install the side panels; they may snap or clip to the back panel. Screw or nail the flanges of the panels to the framing. Install cover moldings over the nails or screws, if required.

Connecting the plumbing

Once you've installed the wall coverings, clean all the surfaces and re-attach the shower head, escutcheons, and faucet handles.

Finally, hang the shower door, or mount a curtain rod and hang a shower curtain.

INSTALLING FIBERGLASS SHOWER PANELS

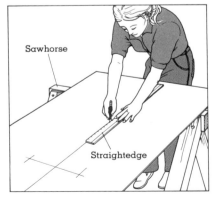

Mark a panel for stubout hole and faucet stem, set panel on supporting planks and sawhorses, and drill holes.

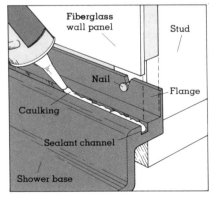

Channel in shower base holds panel tightly in place; sealant prevents moisture from getting behind panels.

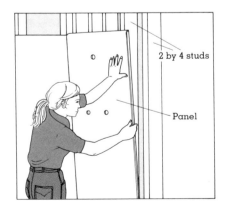

Press panel to the frame, guiding head stubout and faucet stems through holes; nail or screw to frame.

Faucets

Whether you're replacing an old faucet or selecting fittings for a new sink or bathtub, you'll find a wide variety of faucet types and styles to choose from. The product information on page 36 can help you make your selection.

In this section, you'll find information on removing and installing two different types of widely used bathroom faucets: deck-mount models for sinks, and wall-mount models for bathtubs and showers.

SINK FAUCETS

In choosing a deck-mount faucet, be sure that the faucet's inlet shanks are spaced to fit the holes in your sink. If you're replacing a faucet, it's wise to take the old one with you when you shop. You'll also need new water supply lines, so take them with you, too.

Choose a unit that comes with clear installation instructions, and make sure that repair kits or replacement parts are readily available.

Removing a sink faucet

Before removing the faucet, turn off the water at the sink shutoff valves or main shutoff valve. Place a bucket under the valves and use a wrench to remove the coupling nuts connecting the water supply lines to the valves. Open the faucet and allow the water to drain from the lines.

If your sink has a pop-up drain, you'll need to disconnect it before removing the faucet. Unfasten the clevis screw and spring clip that secure the pivot rod to the pop-up rod, and remove the pop-up rod from the faucet body (see drawing on facing page).

With a basin wrench, reach up behind the sink and remove the coupling nuts holding the supply lines to the inlet shanks on the faucet (see illustration above). Now use the basin wrench to remove the locknuts from the shanks. Take off the washers; then lift up the faucet and remove it from the sink or countertop.

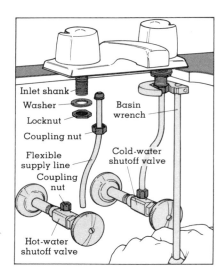

Inlet shank
Washer
Locknut
Coupling nut
Flexible supply line
Coupling nut
Hot-water shutoff valve
Basin wrench
Cold-water shutoff valve

Installing a sink faucet

Before you start, have an adjustable wrench and a basin wrench on hand. If your new faucet doesn't come with a rubber gasket, you'll also need a supply of plumber's putty.

If you're installing a new faucet on an old sink, make sure the area around the faucet is free of dirt and mineral buildup.

The basic steps in installing a sink faucet are outlined below, but since procedures vary with the type of faucet, you should also look carefully at the manufacturer's instructions.

Mounting the faucet. If your new faucet doesn't have a rubber gasket on the bottom, apply a bead of plumber's putty around the underside of the outside edge.

The faucet may have either inlet shanks or attached flexible tubing and threaded stubs. Insert the inlet shanks or tubing down through the holes in the mounting surface and press the faucet onto the surface. For a faucet with inlet shanks, screw the washers and locknuts onto the shanks by hand (see illustration below), then tighten them with a basin wrench. If your faucet has tubing, assemble and tighten the washers and nuts on the threaded studs.

Connecting the plumbing. Two types of flexible supply lines are available: chrome-plated corrugated metal tubing and plastic tubing. Because it's a little better looking, metal tubing is usually used when the supply lines are visible. Gaskets and coupling nuts are sold separately, so be sure they fit the faucet and the shutoff valves. Plastic tubing is sold with gaskets and coupling nuts already assembled.

Before connecting the supply lines, apply pipe joint compound to the threads on the inlet shanks and shutoff valves, or to the threads on the fittings at the ends of the tubing.

INSTALLING A SINK FAUCET

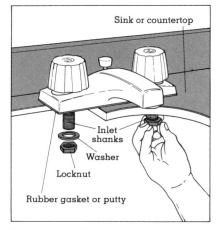

Sink or countertop
Inlet shanks
Washer
Locknut
Rubber gasket or putty

Insert faucet inlet shanks through mounting surface holes, then screw on washers and locknuts.

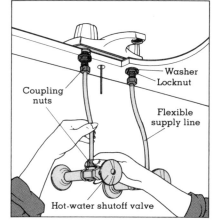

Coupling nuts
Washer
Locknut
Flexible supply line
Hot-water shutoff valve

Attach either metal or plastic flexible supply lines to inlet shanks and to shutoff valves using coupling nuts.

Then connect the supply lines to the inlet shanks or tubes (see illustration on facing page). Tighten the coupling nuts with a basin wrench. Gently bend the supply lines to meet the shutoff valves, and secure them with coupling nuts to the valves. Tighten the nuts with an adjustable wrench, then turn on the water and check for leaks.

If you're installing a new pop-up drain assembly, follow the manufacturer's instructions. Connect the pop-up rod to the new pivot rod, using the fastenings supplied with the new drain assembly.

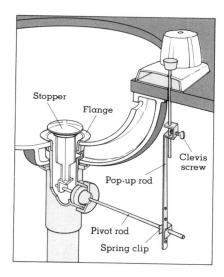

TWO TYPES OF BATHTUB AND SHOWER FAUCETS

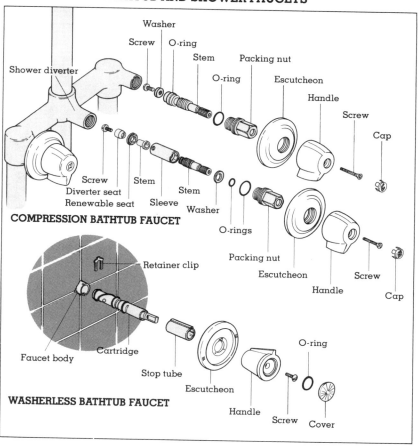

COMPRESSION BATHTUB FAUCET

WASHERLESS BATHTUB FAUCET

BATHTUB & SHOWER FAUCETS

Faucets for bathtubs and showers are either compression models (usually with separate hot and cold water controls) or washerless models (with a single lever or knob to control the flow and mix of hot and cold water). In both types (see illustration above right), the faucet body is mounted directly on the water supply pipes inside the wall.

You can either renovate a bathtub or shower faucet, or completely replace it. If the faucet body is in good condition, you may simply want to replace some of the faucet parts. If the faucet body is in poor condition, or if you can't find new

parts to fit it, you'll have to replace the entire faucet. You'll also need to replace the complete faucet if you want to add a shower head above an existing bathtub (see "Adding a shower faucet," page 110). The following sections tell you how to renovate or replace a faucet.

Renovating a bathtub or shower faucet

To renovate a faucet, you can replace faucet parts—stems, handles, and trim (such as escutcheons)—and the tub spout or shower head. In a tub, you might also replace the diverter—the mechanism that redirects water to the shower pipe. To find the correct replacement parts, it's a good idea to disassemble the old faucet first, then take the parts with you to the store when you shop for new ones.

Before you start work, turn off the water at the bathtub or shower shutoff valves or at the main shutoff valve. (Bathtub or shower shutoff valves may be accessible through a panel in an adjoining room, hall, or closet.)

The drawings on this page show you how typical compression and washerless faucets are put together, but the assembly may vary with individual models. As you disassemble your faucet, take notes and make a sketch of the parts and the sequence of assembly so you'll be able to put the faucet back together. First remove faucet handles, trim, and stem parts; then remove the diverter (if necessary). Finally, remove the tub spout or shower head with a tape-wrapped pipe wrench.

When you're ready to assemble the new fittings, simply reverse the procedure.

(Continued on next page)

. . . Faucets

REMOVING A BATHTUB FAUCET

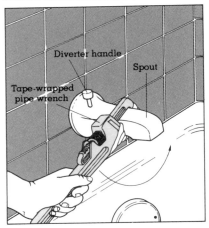

Remove spout from wall stubout by turning counterclockwise with a tape-wrapped pipe wrench.

Remove faucet body from supply pipes by unscrewing or unsoldering the connections.

Replacing a bathtub or shower faucet

Replacing a complete bathtub or shower faucet involves cutting away the wall covering and removing the faucet body from the supply pipes with wrenches or a small propane torch. You'll need to take the old faucet body with you when you buy a new one, to be sure of getting the correct size. If you've never done any pipefitting, you may want to get professional help to install the new faucet body.

Getting to the faucet body. First remove the faucet handles and trim, and the shower head or tub spout and diverter. To work on the faucet body and the pipes behind the wall, open the access door or panel if one is available. If not, cut a hole in the bathroom wall large enough to allow you to work on the faucet body and pipes comfortably (see illustration at right). Then turn off the water at the bathtub shutoff valves or main shutoff valve.

Removing the faucet body. The illustration above shows how a bathtub or shower faucet body is mounted onto the water supply pipes. It may be attached with either threaded or soldered connections. If you find threaded connections, un-

screw them. Use one wrench on the supply pipe to hold it steady, and one wrench on the coupling, turning it counterclockwise. If you find soldered copper connections, unsolder them, using a small propane torch.

Installing the faucet body. If your tub or shower is not equipped with individual shutoff valves, you may want to add them now (consult a professional plumber for help). To install a faucet body on threaded pipe fittings, apply pipe joint compound to the male threads of the pipes and screw the connecting coupling nuts down tight.

For copper pipe, solder couplings to the pipes and screw them onto the faucet body. If the faucet body must be soldered directly to the pipe, first remove the valve and diverter stems.

After the pipes are connected to the faucet body, turn the water on and check for leaks. To make certain the pipes can't vibrate when the water is turned on and off, anchor them and the faucet body firmly to the wall studs or support with pipe straps before patching and re-covering the wall.

Carefully measure and mark the positions of the new faucet, spout, and shower head stubouts on the replacement wall covering. Then

prepare and replace the wall covering, and attach the new fittings.

Adding a shower faucet

If you want to install a shower head in the wall over your bathtub, you'll have to cut into the wall and change the plumbing. You'll need a faucet body that will accept a shower connection and that has a diverter valve to redirect water from tub spout to shower head.

Follow the general procedure for replacing a complete faucet (detailed above), with the following additional steps.

First measure exactly 76 inches above the bottom of the tub and remove all wall covering between two studs, making a hole about 16 inches wide and 60 inches high. Position a 2 by 4 on edge in the opening and toenail it to the studs on both sides of the shower stubout. Then insert the shower pipe and connect it to the faucet body. Secure the top of the pipe to the 2 by 4 with pipe strap, re-cover the wall, and install the shower head.

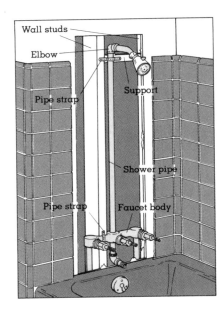

The shower head screws to the shower arm stubout. Before installing it, clean the pipe threads and apply pipe joint compound to the threads to prevent leaks. Tighten the head with a wrench.

Toilets & bidets

Removing or installing a toilet or bidet is not very complicated, especially when the plumbing is already in place. During major remodeling involving the floor or walls, remember that toilets and bidets are the first fixtures to remove and the last to install.

For product information on various models, see page 37.

TOILETS

Conventional two-piece toilets have a floor-mounted bowl with a tank mounted on the bowl. Older types with floor-mounted bowls may have the tank mounted on the wall. One-piece toilets, with the bowl and tank mounted on the floor as a single unit, are becoming increasingly popular with homeowners. (One-piece wall-hung models that connect directly to the stack in the wall are also available.) This section deals primarily with conventional two-piece floor-mounted toilets.

Before you begin work, be sure to check any code requirements for a new or replacement toilet.

Removing a toilet

The procedure for removing a toilet varies with the type of fixture. For a two-piece toilet, you remove the tank first, then the bowl. (For a one-piece toilet, you remove the tank and bowl at the same time.)

Disconnect the water supply. Before you begin work, turn off the water at the fixture shutoff valve or main shutoff valve. Flush the toilet twice to empty the bowl and tank; then sponge out any remaining water. To remove the toilet seat and lid, unfasten the nuts on the two bolts projecting down through the bowl's back edge. Unfasten the coupling nut on the water supply line (see illustration below) underneath the tank. If the line is kinked or corroded, replace it when you install the new toilet.

Remove the tank. If you're removing a bowl-mounted toilet tank, detach the empty tank from the bowl as follows: Locate the mounting bolts inside the tank at the bottom. Hold them stationary with a screwdriver while you use a wrench to unfasten the nuts underneath the tank (see illustration below). You'll find it easier to remove the nuts if a helper holds the screwdriver. Then lift up the tank and remove it.

In a wall-mounted tank, a pipe usually connects the tank and bowl. Loosen the couplings on the pipe and remove it. Then reach inside the tank with a wrench and unscrew the nuts on the hanger bolts—these attach the tank to the hanger bracket on the wall. Now you can remove the tank.

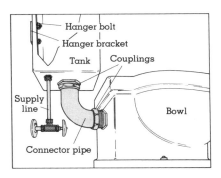

Remove the bowl. The following instructions apply to most floor-mounted toilet bowls. At the base of the bowl near the floor, pry off the caps covering the hold-down floor bolts. Unscrew the nuts from the bolts. If the nuts have rusted on, soak them with penetrating oil or cut the bolts off with a hacksaw.

Gently rock the bowl from side to side, breaking the seal between the bowl and the floor. Lift the bowl straight up, keeping it level so any remaining water doesn't spill from its trap (see illustration below).

Stuff a rag into the open drainpipe to prevent sewer gas from escaping and to keep debris from falling into the opening.

(Continued on next page)

REMOVING A FLOOR-MOUNTED TOILET

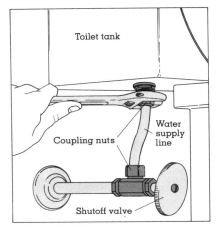

Loosen the coupling nut on the water supply line at the bottom of the tank, using a wrench.

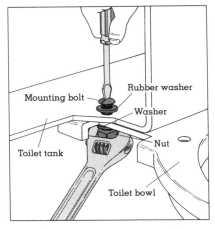

Detach the tank from the bowl by loosening mounting bolts with a screwdriver and a wrench.

Lift the bowl straight up off the floor flange, keeping it level to avoid spilling any remaining water.

... Toilets & bidets

Installing a toilet

The amount of work needed to install a new toilet depends on whether or not it will be in a new location. Hooking up a toilet in a new location is a challenging project because you must extend supply, drain, and vent pipes (pages 89–91). You may want to have a professional run the piping to the desired spot, then complete the installation yourself.

Replacing an old fixture with a new one at the same location is a one-afternoon project that you can do yourself. The only crucial dimension you need to check on a new toilet is its roughing-in size—the distance from the wall to the center of the drainpipe (most are 12 inches).

You can usually determine roughing-in size before removing the old bowl—just measure from the wall to one of the two hold-down bolts that secure the bowl to the floor. (If the bowl has four hold-down bolts, measure to one of the rear bolts.) Your new toilet's roughing-in size can be shorter than that of the fixture you're replacing, but if it's longer, the new toilet won't fit.

Once you've determined that the fixture will fit, you're ready to install it. The following general instructions apply to two-piece floor-mounted toilets. The key steps are illustrated at right. (For a one-piece, floor-mounted toilet, install the bowl as described below, then connect the water supply.)

Prepare the floor flange. This fitting connects the bowl to the floor and drainpipe.

Remove the rags and, with a putty knife, scrape off the wax bowl ring that formed the seal between the bowl and the flange. Thoroughly scrape the flange so that the new ring will form a leakproof seal.

If the old flange is cracked or broken, or if its surface is rough, replace it with a new flange, matched to the existing drainpipe material. (Use a plastic flange with plastic pipe, cast iron with a cast iron pipe.) Remove the old hold-down bolts from the floor flange, then insert the new bolts through the

flange. If necessary, hold them upright with plumber's putty. Align the bolts with the center of the drainpipe.

Install the bowl ring. Turn the new bowl upside down on a cushioned surface. Place the new bowl ring over the toilet horn (outlet) on the bottom of the bowl, and apply plumber's putty around the bowl's bottom edge.

Place the bowl. Check that all packing material has been removed from the new bowl, and all rags from the drainpipe. Then gently lower the

bowl into place over the flange, using the bolts as guides. To form the seal, press down firmly while twisting slightly.

Check the bowl with a level—from side to side and from front to back; use copper or brass washers to shim underneath the bowl where necessary. Be careful not to break the seal. Hand tighten the washers and nuts onto the holddown bolts; you'll tighten them permanently after the tank is in place.

Attach the tank. For a bowl-mounted tank, fit the rubber gasket

INSTALLING A FLOOR-MOUNTED TOILET

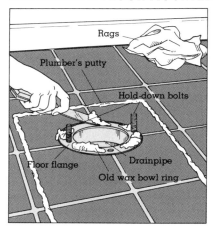

Thoroughly scrape the old bowl ring from the floor flange, using a putty knife or similar tool.

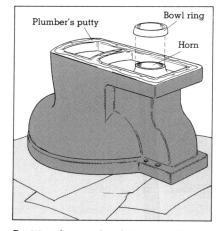

Position the new bowl ring over the toilet horn on the bottom of the bowl as it rests on a cushioned surface.

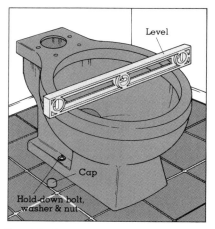

Level the bowl once it's in place, using small copper or brass washers to shim underneath, if necessary.

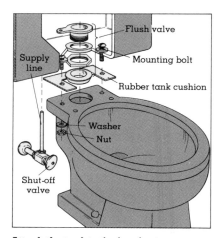

Attach the tank to the bowl using mounting bolts, with rubber gasket and tank cushion in place.

over the end of the flush valve that projects through the bottom of the tank. Place the rubber tank cushion on the rear of the bowl. After positioning the tank on the bowl, insert the mounting bolts through their holes in the bottom of the tank so they pass through the tank cushion and the back of the bowl. Then tighten the nuts and washers onto the bolts. (Secure wall-mounted tanks to hanger brackets with bolts through the back of the tank. Assemble the large pipe between bowl and tank and tighten the couplings.)

Now you can attach the bowl to the floor permanently. Use a wrench to tighten the hold-down nuts at the base of the bowl, but don't overtighten them or you'll crack the bowl. Check to see that the bowl is still level and doesn't rock. Fill the caps with plumber's putty and place them over the nuts. Seal the joint between the base of the bowl and the floor with a bead of caulking compound.

Attach the toilet seat by inserting mounting bolts through the holes in the back of the bowl; then assemble the washers and nuts onto the bolts and tighten.

Connect the plumbing. Connect the water supply line to the underside of the tank. If your old plumbing had no fixture shutoff valve, install one now (consult a professional plumber for help). Finally, turn on the water and check for leaks.

BIDETS

A bidet—a one-piece fixture—is usually installed next to the toilet. Unlike a toilet, a bidet has a sink-type drain and trap and is plumbed for hot and cold water. (For product information, see page 37.)

Removing a bidet

A bidet is usually not difficult to remove. You just disconnect two water supply lines, a drainpipe, and the hold-down bolts.

Disconnect the plumbing. Before doing any work, turn off the

water at the fixture shutoff valves or main shutoff valve. Open all faucets; then unfasten the coupling nuts on the hot and cold water supply lines, so that all remaining water will be completely drained. These lines are either freestanding or attached to the wall behind the bidet. (Some bidets may be plumbed with mixing valves in the wall and a single water supply line running to the fixture.)

Behind and under the back of the bidet you'll find the drainpipe connection and usually a pop-up drain assembly. First, loosen the clevis screw (see illustration on page 109) and disconnect this assembly. Then loosen the slip nuts on the trap and remove it.

Remove the bidet. Pry the caps off the flange at the base of the bidet and remove the nuts underneath them. If the nuts are rusted, soak them with penetrating oil or cut the bolts with a hacksaw.

Lift the bidet straight up off the hold-down bolts that secure it to the floor. You may need to rock the fixture gently first to break the caulk seal (if there is one) around the base.

Stuff a rag into the drainpipe to prevent debris from falling into the opening.

Installing a bidet

A bidet must be mounted to the floor with hold-down bolts. If you're hooking up a new bidet in an existing location and want to use the existing floor bolts, the distance between bolt holes must be the same as for the original fixture. Also make sure the fittings on the new model are compatible with the existing water supply and drain lines.

If you're installing a bidet in a new location, you'll need to extend supply and drainpipes (see pages 88–91). Unless you're experienced in home plumbing, you'll probably want to hire a professional for this part of the job.

Position the bidet. Remove all packing material from the bidet and

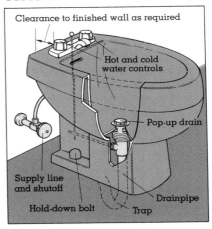

Clearance to finished wall as required

Hot and cold water controls

Pop-up drain

Supply line and shutoff

Hold-down bolt

Drainpipe

Trap

place the fixture so that its drain opening is directly over the drainpipe. If it's a new installation rather than a replacement, mark the locations for the hold-down bolts on the floor, using the holes in the bidet's flange as guides; then remove the bidet, drill holes sized for the bolts, and screw the bolts through the floor. Turn the bidet upside down onto a cushioned surface and apply plumber's putty around the bottom edge.

Remove the rag from the drainpipe and set the bidet back in position, using the bolts as guides.

Level the bidet, from side to side and from front to back, using copper or brass washers to shim beneath the bottom edge, if necessary. If you do shim, you may need to reseal the fixture to the floor. Hand tighten washers and nuts onto the hold-down bolts; you'll tighten them further after the plumbing connections are made. Connect the pop-up drain assembly, if there is one.

Connect the plumbing. Connect the drain and the two water supply lines. Once all connections are made, use a wrench to tighten the nuts on these lines, as well as the nuts on the hold-down bolts. (Don't overtighten the hold-down bolts or you'll crack the fixture.) Fill the caps with plumber's putty and place them over the nuts on the bidet flange. Turn on the water and check for leaks.

Wall coverings

A new moisture-resistant wall covering can give a lift to your bathroom's appearance and make the room easier to maintain at the same time.

This section will show you how to remove and apply three of the most popular wall coverings in today's bathrooms—gypsum wallboard, plastic-coated hardboard panels, and ceramic tile. (For information on painting, see the special feature on page 117.)

GYPSUM WALLBOARD

This versatile wall covering has a gypsum core faced with thick paper. You can use it as finish material, putting paint or wallpaper over it, or you can use it as a backing for other materials, such as tile, wood, or panels of plastic-coated hardboard.

A special water-resistant grade is available for use around tubs, showers, and other damp areas. This wallboard is usually identified by a blue or green paper cover. It's best not to use it where you plan to paint or wallpaper, though—the compound you must use to finish joints between panels of water-resistant wallboard is nearly impossible to sand, so every imperfection will show through.

Panels are generally 4 feet wide and 8 feet long. (Lengths over 8 feet can be specially ordered.) Common thicknesses are ⅜ inch for wallboard used as a backing, ½ inch for wallboard used as finish wall covering.

Removing gypsum wallboard

If your bathroom's existing wallboard has only minor cracks or holes, you can probably repair it (see "Repairing gypsum wallboard," page 116). But if it's wet, mildewed, or badly damaged, you'll have to remove it before installing other wall covering.

Use a broad-bladed prybar and claw hammer to remove wallboard. Wear a painter's mask to avoid inhaling gypsum dust, and cover all fixtures and the floor with drop cloths. Finally, be sure to turn off electrical power to the bathroom by flipping a circuit breaker or removing a fuse, so you won't risk hitting a live wire with the prybar.

Your wallboard may be nailed at intervals along the wall studs, or nailed only around the outside edges and sealed to the studs with adhesive. In either case, the removal procedure is the same.

Break through a taped seam between panels with the prybar. Then pry up the panel, using the stud for leverage, until you loosen a large piece. With both hands, pull the piece of wallboard off the studs. (Some of the nails will probably come off with it.) If the wallboard is attached with adhesive, you can leave the backing paper on the studs.

Once you've completely stripped the wallboard away from the studs, work through the area a second time and pull out any remaining nails.

Installing gypsum wallboard

Installing gypsum wallboard is a three-step procedure. You measure and cut panels to size, hang them, and finish the seams and corners with wallboard compound and tape. Handle bulky panels carefully as you work; take care not to bend or break corners or tear the paper covers.

Cut the wallboard. Though you'll use some full-size panels, you'll also need to cut pieces to fit around doors, windows, fixtures, and cabinets.

To make a straight, simple cut, first mark a line on the front of the panel with a pencil and straightedge, or snap a chalk line. Cut through the front paper with a utility knife; use a straightedge to guide the knife. Break the gypsum core by bending the board toward the back, as shown in the drawing below. Finally, cut the paper on the back along the bend. Smooth the cut edge with a perforated rasp.

To fit wallboard around doors, windows, and other openings, measure and mark carefully. Measure from vertical edges of the opening to the edge of the nearest panel or a corner; measure from horizontal edges to the floor. Transfer the measurements to the wallboard and make the cutout with a keyhole saw. For mid-panel cutouts, drill a pilot hole, then use a keyhole saw to make the cutout.

CUTTING GYPSUM WALLBOARD

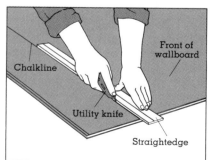

Cut wallboard along pencil or chalk line marked on front face, using utility knife guided by straightedge.

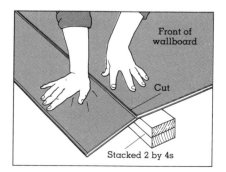

Break gypsum core by placing edges of stacked 2 by 4s under cut and pressing down on panel.

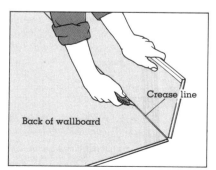

Complete cut by turning panel over, bending wallboard back, and cutting through back paper with utility knife.

HANGING WALLBOARD PANELS

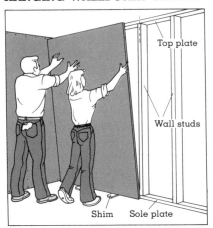

Position a wallboard panel by pushing it up slowly and centering each panel edge over a stud.

Nail wallboard panel along top and bottom and into each stud, dimpling panel surface without puncturing it.

Hang the panels. Before installing panels, make sure the wall studs are plumb and flat. Mark stud locations on the floor and ceiling (16 or 24 inches on center is the usual spacing for studs). Center each panel edge over a stud and nail it to the stud with wallboard nails. Also nail the panel to the top and sole plates (see illustration above) and to the studs behind it (this is called "field" nailing). The spacing of nails, both along panel edges and "in the field," is specified by local building codes. Drive in all nails with a smooth-faced hammer, so that the hammer dimples the panel surface without puncturing the paper.

Wallboard that will be backing for some kinds of tile can be fastened to studs with adhesive and nailed only at the top and bottom plates.

Tape the joints and corners. If your wallboard will be a backing for paneling, you won't need to tape and conceal joints or corners. But if you're painting, wallpapering, or installing tile, you must finish the wallboard carefully. You'll need these basic tools and materials: 6 and 10-inch taping knives, a corner tool, sandpaper, wallboard tape, and taping compound (water-resistant wallboard requires water-resistant compound). See NOTE,

below, for special instructions on tapping water-resistant wallboard.

Finishing is done in stages over a period of days. To tape a joint between panels, first apply a smooth layer of taping compound over the joint with a 6-inch taping knife. Before the compound dries, use the knife to embed wallboard tape into it, and apply another thin coat of compound over the tape, smoothing it gently with the knife.

Tape and finish all joints between panels in the same manner. Then, with smooth, even strokes of the 6-inch knife, cover the nail dimples in the field with compound.

Allow the taping compound to dry for at least 24 hours; then sand lightly until the surface is smooth. Wear a face mask and goggles while sanding, and make sure the room is well ventilated.

Now use a 10-inch knife to apply a second coat of compound, extending it a few inches on each side of the taped joint. Feather the compound out toward the edges.

Let the second coat dry, sand it, then apply a final coat. Use the 10-inch knife to smooth out and feather the edges, covering all dimples and joints. Once the compound dries, sand it again to remove even minor imperfections.

NOTE: To finish water-resistant wallboard that will be backing for ceramic tile, follow a slightly different procedure. First embed the tape in water-resistant taping compound

TAPING WALLBOARD JOINTS

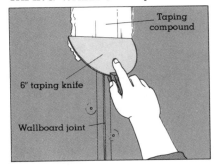

Apply a smooth layer of taping compound over wallboard joint, using a 6-inch taping knife.

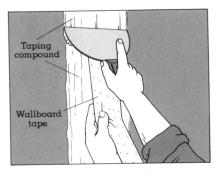

Embed wallboard tape into the compound before it dries, and apply another thin layer of compound.

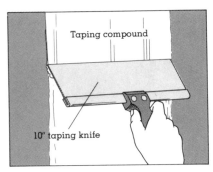

Apply a second coat a few inches on each side of joint, feathering compound out to edges.

. . . Wall coverings

along panel joints; then remove all excess compound with a taping knife. Apply a second thin coat over the wet taping coat and fill any nail dimples. Do not leave excess compound—it can't be sanded dry.

To tape an inside corner, use special precreased tape. Apply a smooth layer of compound to the wallboard on each side of the corner. Measure and tear the tape, fold it in half vertically along the prepared crease, and press it into the corner with a corner tool. Apply a thin layer of compound over the tape and smooth it out with a corner tool (see illustration below); then finish as you did the other joints.

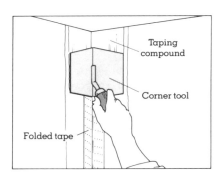

Nail metal cornerbeads to all exterior corners to protect them. Apply compound to each side of the corner with a 6-inch knife. When it's dry, sand it smooth. With a 10-inch knife, apply a second coat of compound, feathering it. Allow to dry, then sand away imperfections.

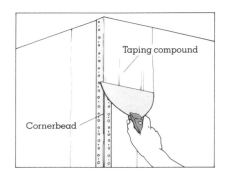

Repairing gypsum wallboard

To determine whether the gypsum wallboard that's already in your bathroom can be used for backing or finished wall covering, inspect each panel for holes and cracks. If the damage is not great, you can probably repair the panels rather than replace them. Before doing any other work, make any necessary repairs as described below.

Small holes and cracks. Before patching small cracks and holes (such as nail holes), brush them clean and dampen the wall surface around them. (Better still, seal the area with shellac and let it dry.) Then use a flexible narrow-bladed putty knife to fill the holes with a tiny amount of ready-mixed spackling compound.

Sand all patched areas until they're smooth. If you'll be repainting with a light-colored paint, prime the patches with the paint so they won't show through later.

Large holes and cracks. Using a sharp utility knife or hacksaw blade, cut a neat rectangle around the hole or crack in the wall (see drawing below). Then, from another piece of wallboard, cut a patch 1 inch wider on all sides than the rectangle you've cut out of the wall.

Lay the new patch of wallboard front-side down on a flat surface. With the knife, cut a plug the same size as the wall's rectangle *without* scoring the paper on the front side of the wallboard. Remove an inch of board from around the sides of the patch, leaving a 1-inch margin of the front paper on all four sides.

Spread a thin layer of spackling or taping compound around and on the edges of the hole in the wall. Position the patch and press it into the hole until it's even with the wall surface. Cover the seams and entire surface with spackling or taping compound. Let it dry, then smooth it with sandpaper.

If your walls have cracks that continually reappear because of structural expansion and contraction, try using special crack patcher—a combination of pliable coating material and flexible bridging fabric. Crack patcher "gives" with further house movement so cracks don't reappear. To apply, follow the manufacturer's instructions.

For minor gaps between wallboard and an adjacent surface such as a window frame, simply use a caulking gun to seal the gap with latex caulking compound.

(Continued on page 118)

REPAIRING HOLES IN WALLBOARD

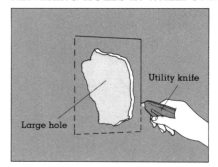

Cut a neat rectangle around the hole to be patched, using a sharp utility knife or a hacksaw blade.

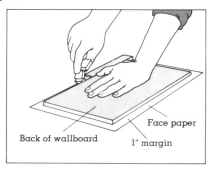

Make rectangular patch an inch wider on all sides; remove an inch from margins, leaving face paper intact.

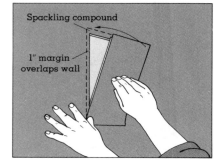

Apply spackle or taping compound around edges of the hole, and press into it the finished patch with paper border.

PAINTING: TIPS FOR A PROFESSIONAL FINISH

A fresh coat of paint is the fastest way to brighten up your bathroom. Here are some guidelines to help you do a professional-looking job.

Selecting tools & materials

One key to a good paint job is to choose the right materials.

Paint. Your best choice is an oil-base alkyd enamel in either a gloss or satin finish. Alkyds, which have largely replaced traditional oil-base paints, are just what you need in a moist bathroom environment. They're moisture and mildew-resistant and washable, and they have good color retention and sticking power. An excellent choice for woodwork is interior/exterior, quick-drying alkyd enamel; it has a brilliant, tilelike finish that's extremely durable.

Tools. Though natural bristle brushes are traditionally used to apply oil-base alkyd enamel paints, you can also use brushes with synthetic bristles. For window sashes and trim, choose a 1½ or 2-inch angled sash brush. A 2 or 3-inch brush or a paint pad is best for woodwork, doors, and cabinets.

For walls, ceilings, and most paneling, a 3½ or 4-inch brush may be used—but for a quick and easy job, a roller is the answer. A 9-inch roller will handle a bathroom of any size. If you'll be painting the ceiling, get a roller with a threaded handle to accommodate an extension pole.

Preparing the surface

To prevent cracking and peeling after the new paint dries, you must begin with surfaces that are smooth and clean.

It's possible to paint over wallpaper that's smooth and attached firmly to the wall. Apply a sealing primer such as pigmented shellac or a flat oil-base enamel undercoat. Let the sealer dry completely before you paint. It's often safer, though, to remove the wallpaper, especially if it's tearing and flaking.

Repairing the finish. For an old painted finish, sanding is sufficient if the surface is flaking lightly. Wash dirty areas on wood surfaces before sanding.

Roughen glossy paint surfaces with sandpaper so the new paint will adhere. (Rough, bare wood also needs sanding, as do patched areas.)

When a wood finish is in such bad condition that painting over it is impossible, you'll have to strip it. You can use an electric paint softener or heat gun, or a commercial liquid paint remover. With either method, you take off the softened paint with a broad knife or scraper, then sand the surface lightly until it's clean and smooth.

Once you've prepared the surface, carefully inspect it for small holes and cracks.

To repair gypsum wallboard, see the facing page. For information on repairing other surfaces, consult a wall covering specialist.

Finally, dust everything in the bathroom, then vacuum the floor. With an abrasive cleaner, sponge the areas you plan to paint, then rinse. Allow about 24 hours for all washed areas to dry completely.

Prime the surface. Before doing any finish painting, be sure to prime the surface. Use the primer recommended by the paint manufacturer for the type of surface you'll be painting.

Applying the paint

To avoid painting yourself into a corner, you'll want to follow the working sequence outlined below.

Ceiling. If you're painting both ceiling and walls, begin with the ceiling. Paint the entire surface in one session. It's best to paint in 2 by 3-foot rectangles, starting in a corner and working across the shortest dimension of the ceiling.

On the first section, use a brush or special corner pad to paint a narrow strip next to the wall line and around any fixtures. Then finish the section with a roller, overlapping any brush marks. Work your way back and forth across the ceiling, painting one section at a time. Then go on to the walls.

Walls. Mentally divide a wall into 3-foot-square sections, starting from a corner at the ceiling line and working down the wall. As with ceilings, paint the edges of each section first with a brush or corner roller. Paint along the ceiling line and corners, and around fixtures and edges of doors or windows. Finish each section with a roller or brush, overlapping any brush marks.

At the bottom of the walls above the floor or baseboard, and along the edges of vanities and medicine cabinets, use a brush and painting guide to get a neat, even edge. Be sure to overlap any remaining brush marks with your roller.

As a final step, return to the ceiling line and again work down in 3-foot sections.

. . . Wall coverings

PLASTIC-COATED HARDBOARD PANELS

Because they're water-resistant and tough, plastic-coated hardboard panels are a popular bathroom wall covering. They come in a variety of decorative finishes, from wood-grain to plain colors. You can install them as floor-to-ceiling wall covering or as wainscoting.

Available in 4 by 8-foot sheets, the panels are ⅛ or ¼ inch thick. They're made to fit into slotted metal or plastic molding that holds them to the wall and to each other. Corner moldings and divider strips join panels together; cap moldings finish panel edges.

Removing hardboard panels

To remove hardboard panels from bathroom walls, you'll follow the same general procedure used to remove fiberglass shower panels (see pages 105–106). The gypsum wallboard backing will usually come off with them. You'll have to replace the wallboard before installing most kinds of new panels.

Installing hardboard panels

When you install new plastic-coated hardboard panels, you may be able to use the existing walls as backing. The wall covering may be wallboard or plaster, or even panels of fiberglass, plastic, or wood. Whatever the material, the walls must be clean, smooth, flat, and dry. Check the panel manufacturer's installation instructions.

Make a drawing. Draw your bathroom wall plan to scale, noting the locations of all fixtures and accessories. Plan the placement of full and partial panels so there's a minimum of waste. The joints between panels should be located over studs. Determine how many full panels to order, and the types of molding you'll need to secure the panels.

Prepare the walls. Once you've decided where the panels and moldings will be installed, remove all fixtures, baseboards, and ceiling moldings. Prepare the backing surface according to the panel manufacturer's instructions.

Next, use a level to mark horizontal top or bottom guidelines for placing the panels on the backing. Use a plumb bob or level to mark vertical joints. When marking guidelines for panels used as wainscoting, note that the usual height for a wainscot is 48 inches above the floor.

Cut moldings and panels. Cut the moldings and partial panels to size. Use a hacksaw and miter box when you cut the moldings, and file down any rough edges.

Cut panels finished-side up with a fine-tooth handsaw, or face-down with a portable circular saw. (Support face-down panels on a padded surface to avoid scratching them.) Sand all rough edges. To cut openings for fixtures and accessories, use a saber saw on face-down panels. Bevel the panels' back edges with a plane so they'll fit more easily into the moldings.

Attach panels. Prepare moldings and divider strips by punching or drilling nail holes along their flanges. You'll caulk along the vertical joint lines marked on the backing; then nail moldings with 3-penny or 4-penny box nails.

Prepare each panel just before you're ready to install it. Position it face-down on two padded sawhorses, and apply the adhesive recommended by the manufacturer to the back with a notched spreader.

The sequence you'll follow to attach panels and moldings varies with your bathroom's size and layout, and the panel manufacturer's recommendations. You may begin at a corner, by a doorway, or in the middle of a wall.

Generally, you'll nail divider strips to the backing first, then fit panel edges into their slots. Corners get different treatment. At an inside

INSTALLING PLASTIC-COATED PANELS

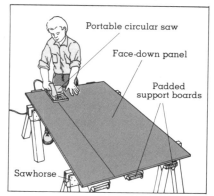

To cut a plastic-coated hardboard panel lengthwise, set it on two sawhorses face-down and use a portable circular saw.

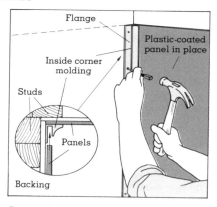

Set inside corner molding in place over adjoining panel and in caulking, then nail to stud with 4-penny box nails.

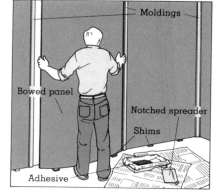

Apply adhesive to panel back, then slip between moldings, bowing panel out at center. Hold against ceiling with shims.

corner, a panel must be installed on one wall (see illustration below left) before you can nail up the corner molding. Once the molding is nailed on, you can slip the panel for the adjoining wall into the molding slot.

When you install a full panel between two divider strips, fit in one edge first, then bow the panel toward you at the center so you can slip the other edge into its slot (see illustration). Narrow panels won't bow, however. You'll have to slip one edge into a molding nailed to the backing, place a divider strip over the other edge, and then press both strip and panel onto the backing at the same time. Once the panel and strip are in place, nail the exposed flange of the divider strip into the backing. (Use the same basic method to attach a wainscot and top cap molding. An alternative is to attach cap molding to the wall, then slip the wainscot's top edge into the molding.)

When you attach a panel, press it firmly against the backing to ensure a tight bond. Use shims under panels if needed to make them level and to hold them against the ceiling (or top cap molding for a wainscot). As soon as possible, clean any adhesive off the panel faces with solvent.

After you've installed all panels, you may want to add narrow wood molding at the ceiling line for floor-to-ceiling panels, and baseboards along the floor.

CERAMIC TILE

Few wall coverings have the decorative impact and durability of ceramic tile. It's a natural choice for any wall that might be sprayed or splashed—water, dirt, and soap film clean away in seconds.

On these pages you'll learn how to remove and install ceramic tile on your bathroom walls. For information on various types of wall tile, see page 39. If your plans call for a ceramic tile floor, install the floor tiles before setting tiles on the wall (see page 124).

Removing ceramic tile

Removing wall tile set in mortar is a tough job. If possible, replace only those tiles that are damaged. If tiles are clean and smooth and the wall surface is flat, consider installing the new tiles directly over them.

If you must remove old tile, proceed with caution (see "Removing the wall covering" on page 105). It's best to have a professional remove tile that is set in mortar.

If your wall tile is set on gypsum wallboard, you can more easily remove it yourself. Wearing goggles and a painter's mask, use a cold chisel and soft-headed steel hammer to chip through the tile and backing. Once you've removed small sections, insert a prybar and pry off large sections until the wall studs are exposed.

Inspect the exposed wall framing for water damage, and replace framing members if necessary. Then install new water-resistant wallboard as backing for new tile, or another wall covering of your choice.

Installing ceramic tile

Plan and prepare carefully before you install tile. First measure your bathroom and sketch your walls on graph paper. Choose and plan the placement of special trim pieces, such as bullnose, cove, and quarter-round edging tiles, as well as ceramic accessories—soap dishes, paper holders, and toothbrush holders. Your dealer can help you to select trim pieces.

Once you've designed your walls and selected tile, you're ready to begin. Described below are the steps you'll follow to install your tile, from backing to finished wall. (If you're installing pregrouted tile panels, follow the manufacturer's instructions.)

Before you start, remove baseboards and window and door trim, wall-mounted accessories and lights, and if necessary, the toilet, bidet, and sink.

Prepare the backing surface. This is probably the most important

step in installing wall tile successfully. Backing must be solid, flat, clean, and dry.

You may use new or existing gypsum wallboard or even existing wood or tile as backing if it's in good condition. Clean off all dirt and grease. Repair old tile and use an abrasive disc mounted on an electric drill to clean and roughen the surface for better adhesion. Remove old finish from wood and sand it smooth. Check the wall covering's surface with a straightedge; if it's irregular, you may be able to level it with a mastic underlayment or another compound recommended by the tile adhesive manufacturer (see below).

You may need to prime or seal new or existing wallboard backing. A primer or sealer (also called a bonderizer) penetrates the backing to increase water resistance and strengthen the bond between the backing and the new tile. Again, check the adhesive manufacturer's recommendations.

You can select one of three types of thin-set adhesive—organic-based or cement-based (the two most commonly used types), or epoxy-based. Read the label and consult your tile dealer to determine which kind to use with your materials.

Once your backing is prepared, you're ready to mark working lines and set wall tile.

Mark working lines. Accurate horizontal and vertical working lines help you keep tiles properly aligned so that your finished wall will look level and even. The horizontal working line should be near the bottom of the wall, because tiling up a wall is easier than tiling down.

If you're tiling around a tub, establish working lines there first. This way, you can plan for a row of full (uncut) tiles just above the tub, at bathers' eye level. This works out best if the tub is level to within ⅛ inch. Locate the high point of the tub lip with your level, and measure up one tile width plus ⅛ inch. Mark a level line on the wall through this point; then extend it carefully across

... Wall coverings

all adjoining walls. This will give you a bottom row of full tiles around the tub. (You can fill in any small gaps below them with caulking later.)

If your tub is not level to within ⅛ inch, locate the horizontal working line from the low point of the tub lip, and follow the above method. You'll have to cut the bottom row of tiles to fit.

Then, on walls adjoining the tub, establish a line close to the floor. Start at the working line you extended from the tub wall and measure down a full number of tiles, including grout joints. Leave a space at least one full tile high above the floor. Mark the horizontal working line for this wall through this point with a straightedge and level (see illustration below).

To establish a line on a wall not adjoining a tub, find the lowest point by setting a level on the floor at various locations against the walls to be tiled. At the lowest point, place a tile against the wall and mark its top edge on the wall. If you're installing a cove base, set a cove tile on the floor and a wall tile above it (allow for grout joint); then mark the top of the wall tile. Using a level and straightedge, draw a horizontal line through the mark across the wall. Extend this line onto other walls to be tiled.

After marking your horizontal working lines, nail battens (1 by 2

inch wood strips) all along the walls with their top edges on the lines. These will be your horizontal guides.

To establish a vertical working line, locate the midpoint of a wall and mark it on the horizontal working line. Starting at this point, set up a row of loose tiles on the batten to see how they'll fit at the ends of the wall.

If you'll end up with less than half a tile on both ends, move your mark one-half a tile to the right or left to avoid ending the rows with narrow pieces. Then extend the vertical working line through your mark and up the wall with a straightedge and level (see illustration below).

If you don't plan to tile to the ceiling line, mark the point where the highest tile will be set. Using a level, draw a horizontal line through this point across the wall.

PATTERNS FOR SETTING TILE

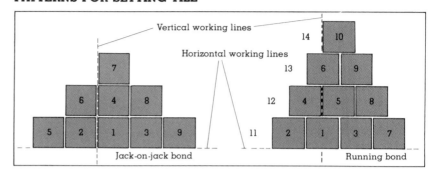

Finally, be sure to mark locations of ceramic towel bars, soap dishes, and other accessories.

Set the tile. First, prepare the tile adhesive according to the manufacturer's directions. (Be sure to keep your working area well ventilated.)

To determine how large an area to cover at one time, consult the adhesive container label for the open time—the length of time you have to work with the adhesive after spreading. Comb the adhesive with a notched trowel to form ridges.

When you set the tiles, place each one with a slight twist—don't slide it. Keep spacing for grout joints uniform. Some tiles have small ceramic spacing lugs molded onto their edges; if your tiles don't have them, drive 6-penny finishing nails into the wallboard to act as temporary spacing guides (see illustration on facing page).

The way you'll begin setting tiles depends on which bond you use—jack-on-jack (with joints lined up) or running bond (with staggered joints).

For jack-on-jack, set the first tile on the batten so that one side is aligned exactly with the vertical working line. Set additional tiles as shown in the illustration above, forming a pyramid pattern. For running bond, *center* the first tile on the vertical working line, then follow the pyramid pattern (illustrated above), as you set the tile.

With either bond, continue setting tiles upward and toward the ends of the wall in the pattern illustrated. After laying several tiles, set

WORKING LINES FOR TILE

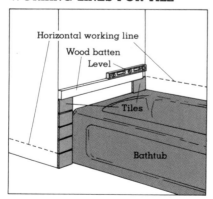

Extend horizontal working line around tub to adjoining walls, then measure to floor. Extend lines along adjoining walls.

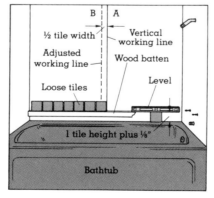

To establish vertical working line, locate midpoint of wall (A), then adjust (B) according to size of end tiles.

them into the adhesive by sliding a carpet-wrapped piece of plywood across the tiles as you tap it gently with a hammer.

Cut tiles to fit at the end of each horizontal row and at the top near the ceiling. (Use a rented tile cutter to cut straight pieces; use tile nippers to cut out irregular shapes.) For the top row of a wainscoting or other installation that doesn't reach the ceiling, set bullnose or cap tiles.

When you come to a wall where there are electrical outlets or switches, turn off the power to them. Remove the cover plates and pull the outlets and switches from their boxes, but don't disconnect them. Cut and fit tiles around the boxes, then remount the outlets and switches.

On inside corners, butt tiles together. On outside corners, set one column of bullnose tiles to cover the unfinished edges of the tiles on each adjoining wall.

INSTALLING WALL TILE

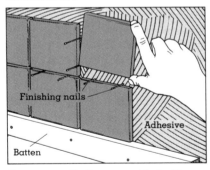

To space wall tiles not molded with spacing lugs, place 6-penny finishing nails between tiles.

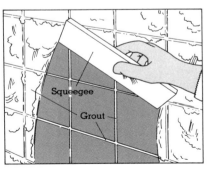

Spread grout on tile, forcing it into joints with a float or squeegee until they're full. Remove excess.

Around windows, finish off the sides and sill with bullnose tiles cut to fit.

Install ceramic accessories such as soap dishes in spaces you left open when tiling. Tape the accessories in place while the adhesive sets.

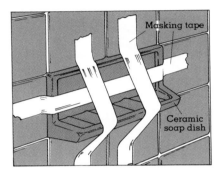

Now check your work. If anything is out of alignment, wiggle it into position before the adhesive sets. Clean adhesive from the face of

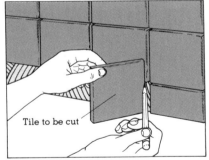

To set bottom row of tiles, remove batten on working line, mark tile and cut. Set in adhesive as for other tiles.

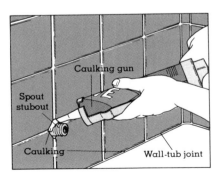

Use bathtub caulk to seal all openings between fixtures or pipes and tile.

tiles and accessories, and from joint spaces.

When the adhesive has set, carefully remove the battens. Twist nail spacers as you pull them out from the wall.

Spread adhesive at the bottom of the wall where the battens were, and set the remaining tiles, cutting them as needed.

Grout the tile. Allow the adhesive to set properly—usually you must allow 16 hours for epoxy-based, 24 hours for organic-based, and 48 hours for cement-based adhesive.

Remove any excess adhesive from the tile joints. Then mix the grout recommended for your tile, and spread it on the surface of the tile with a rubber-faced float or a squeegee, forcing it into the tile joints until they're completely filled. Scrape off excess grout from the tile, working diagonally across the surface.

Wipe the tiles with a wet sponge to remove any remaining grout. Rinse and wring out the sponge frequently, wiping until the grout joints are smooth and level with the tile surface. When the tiles are as clean as you can get them, let the grout dry until a haze appears over the surface. Then polish the haze off the tiles with a soft cloth. Finish (tool) the joints with the end of a toothbrush handle.

Seal tile and grout. Installations with unglazed tile or with cement-based grouts need to be protected by a grout and tile sealer. Most sealers for bathroom tile have a silicone base.

Follow manufacturer's instructions for applying these sealers. Both tiles and grout should be dry. On new tile, wait at least 2 weeks—this will give the grout a chance to cure completely. Apply a moderate amount of sealer, and wipe off any excess to prevent the tile from discoloring.

Finally, use caulking to seal all openings or gaps between pipes or fixtures and tile. Replace all trim, accessories, and fixtures.

Flooring

Two requirements for bathroom floors are moisture resistance and durability. Resilient sheet flooring and ceramic tile are ideal choices on both counts. If you're completely remodeling your bathroom, it's a good time to put in ceramic tile, since it's ideally installed with vanity cabinets, doors, and fixtures removed from the room. If you're replacing only the floor, resilient flooring is a good choice; it can be installed *around* most fixtures and cabinets.

RESILIENT SHEET FLOORING

Resilient sheet flooring is available with smooth or textured surfaces, in plain colors or in patterns. The patterns include authentic-looking imitations of all types of flooring, from wood to ceramic tile.

Though a few types are available in widths up to 12 feet, most sheet flooring is only 6 feet wide, so seams may be necessary.

Removing resilient flooring

You may be able to install new flooring over an existing resilient sheet floor (see "Prepare the subfloor" at right). If you must remove the old flooring, first cut it into strips using a utility or linoleum knife. Be sure you cut through the flooring only, not into the subfloor. Then, as you pass a propane torch or old steam iron over the flooring surface to soften the adhesive underneath, peel or scrape

the strips off the subfloor with a wide putty knife or floor scraper. Finally, scrape off any remaining adhesive or backing from the subfloor.

Check the subfloor for water damage or dry rot, and replace it if necessary.

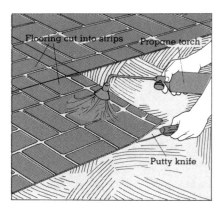

Installing resilient flooring

The information in this section assumes that your floor is supported by a standard subfloor, with joists or beams below (see illustration on page 83). If your home is built on a cement slab and your flooring will be installed over it, you need to make sure that the slab is dry, level, and clean before you begin any work (consult a contractor if you need help inspecting your slab).

Plan the new floor. Take exact measurements of the floor and make a scale drawing. Include the locations of doorways, fixtures, vanities, and any irregularities.

To cover a large bathroom, it may be necessary to seam two pieces together. Looking at your floor plan, decide how to combine sheets so you cover the floor with the minimum waste of material. If the flooring is patterned, remember that you'll need enough material to match the pattern at the seams.

Prepare the subfloor. Old resilient or wood flooring both make acceptable bases for new resilient sheets, provided their surfaces are completely smooth and level. Old resilient flooring must be solid, not cushioned, and firmly bonded to the subfloor. Uneven wood floors may need a rough sanding. Both types must be thoroughly cleaned, and any loose tiles or boards must be secured.

If the old floor is cushioned or in poor condition, it should be removed down to the subfloor, if possible (see "Removing resilient flooring" at left). If the old flooring is impossible to remove without damaging the subfloor, or if the subfloor is in poor condition, cover the old flooring with ¼-inch underlayment-grade plywood or untempered hardboard. (If there are signs of water damage or insect infestation, though, you should consult a professional.)

Cut the flooring. The most critical step in laying sheet flooring is making the first rough cuts accurately. You may want your flooring dealer to make these first cuts for you; if so, you'll need to supply a floor plan.

INSTALLING RESILIENT FLOORING WITH SEAM

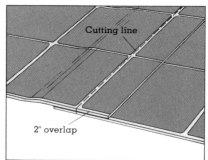

Position second sheet of flooring so it overlaps first sheet by at least 2 inches. Make sure that any patterns match.

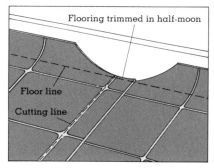

Trim away excess flooring, a little at a time, in a half-moon shape so ends butt against wall.

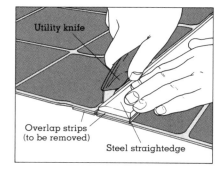

Make a straight cut down through both sheets of flooring, using a utility knife and straightedge.

To cut the flooring to size yourself, unroll the material in a large room or in a clean garage or basement. Transfer the floor plan directly onto the new flooring, using chalk or a water-soluble felt-tip pen, a carpenter's square, and a long straightedge.

If your flooring will have a seam, be sure to allow for overlap or for matching the pattern (if any) on adjoining sheets. If your flooring has simulated grout or mortar joints, cut the seam along the midpoint of the joint.

Using a linoleum or utility knife, cut the flooring so it's roughly 3 inches oversize on all sides (the excess will be trimmed away after the flooring has been put in place).

If a seam is necessary, cut and install the piece of flooring that requires the most intricate fitting first; then cut and install the second sheet.

Install the flooring. Following are instructions for laying resilient sheet flooring—both with and without seams—using adhesive. Some types of sheet flooring can also be laid *without* adhesive. In this case, you simply roll out the flooring and shift it until it's in the proper position, then apply adhesive around the edges or staple the edges in place. If you're considering this easy installation method, check with your flooring dealer to be sure the material you've selected doesn't require adhesive.

If you're installing a single piece of flooring, you can spread adhesive over the entire subfloor at once, or spread adhesive in steps as the flooring is unrolled. Check the adhesive's open time (the time you have to work with the adhesive while it's still tacky); follow the directions of the adhesive manufacturer.

If the entire floor has been covered with adhesive, slowly roll the flooring out across the floor, taking care to set the flooring firmly into the adhesive as you go. If you're working a section at a time, spread adhesive and unroll the flooring as you go.

If you're installing flooring with seams, spread the adhesive on the subfloor as directed by the adhesive manufacturer, but stop 8 or 9 inches from the seam. Then position the first sheet on the floor.

Next, position the second sheet of flooring carefully so that it overlaps the first sheet by at least 2 inches (see illustrations under "Installing resilient flooring with seam," on facing page); make sure the design is perfectly aligned. Then roll up the flooring and spread adhesive over the remainder of the floor, stopping 8 or 9 inches from the edge of the first sheet of flooring. Reposition the second sheet of flooring, starting at the seam; again, take care to align the design perfectly. Then roll the flooring out, setting it into the adhesive.

When the flooring is in position, trim away excess flooring at each end of the seam in a half-moon shape so ends butt against wall.

Using a steel straightedge and a sharp utility knife, make a straight cut (about ½ to ⅝ inch from the edge of the top sheet) down through both sheets of flooring. Lift up the flooring on either side of the seam, remove the two overlap strips (see illustration on facing page), and spread adhesive on subfloor under the seam.

Use the recommended solvent to clean adhesive from around the seam. When the seam is dry and clean, use the recommended seam sealer to fuse the two pieces.

Trim to fit. When the flooring has been positioned, you'll need to make a series of relief cuts at all corners so the flooring will lie flat (see illustrations under "Trimming resilient flooring," below).

At outside corners, start at the top of the excess flooring and cut straight down to the point where the wall and floor meet. At inside corners, cut the excess flooring away a little at a time until it lies flat in the corner.

To remove the excess flooring along a wall, press the flooring into a right angle where the floor and wall join, using an 18 to 24-inch-long piece of 2 by 4. Then lay a heavy metal straightedge along the wall and trim the flooring with a utility knife, leaving a gap of about ⅛ inch between the edge of the flooring and the wall to allow the material to expand without buckling.

(Continued on next page)

TRIMMING RESILIENT FLOORING

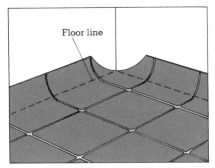

To trim inside corners, cut excess flooring away a little at a time until flooring lies flat in corner.

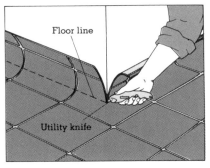

To trim outside corners, use utility knife to cut straight down to where wall and floor meet.

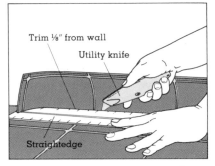

To trim along walls, cut flooring with a utility knife and straightedge, leaving a ⅛-inch gap for expansion.

. . . Flooring

CERAMIC TILE FLOORING

Installing a new floor of ceramic tile can be a very satisfying do-it-yourself project. New, easy-to-install tiles and improved adhesives and grouts make it possible for a careful, patient do-it-yourselfer to create a floor of professional quality.

Because it's usually possible to use existing ceramic tile as a subfloor (see "Prepare the subfloor," below), this section covers installation only—not removal. It's not easy to remove an old tile floor, particularly if the tiles were laid in mortar. So if removal is necessary, it's best to consult a professional.

Installing a ceramic tile floor is essentially a three-step operation: you lay evenly spaced tiles in a bed of adhesive atop a properly prepared subfloor, fill the joint spaces between tiles with grout, and seal the floor for durability and easy cleaning. In this section you'll find basic instructions for laying tile flooring; if you need more detailed information, turn to a contractor or your tile supplier.

Prepare the subfloor. Ceramic tile, masonry, wood, and resilient (except the cushion type) floors can be successfully covered with ceramic tile—provided the old floor is well-bonded, level, clean, and dry.

If the existing flooring is in poor condition, you'll need to repair, cover, or remove it before you can proceed. Fasten loose ceramic, masonry, or resilient flooring with adhesive; nail down loose wood flooring; fill gouges in resilient flooring; and sand wood floors smooth.

If the old floor is beyond repair—or if it's a cushioned resilient floor—it should be removed down to the subfloor, if possible. (Instructions for removing resilient sheet flooring appear on page 122.) If the old flooring is impossible to remove without damaging the subfloor, or if the subfloor is in poor condition, cover the old flooring with ¼-inch underlayment-grade plywood or untempered hardboard.

Your tile dealer can recommend the best adhesive for your new tile floor (the type of adhesive depends on the type of flooring you'll be covering). Follow your dealer's instructions for preparing the subfloor, and be sure to check the directions on the adhesive container, as well.

Establish working lines. The key to laying straight rows of tile is to first establish accurate working lines. Following are instructions for laying out working lines starting from the center of the room. This method makes it easy to keep rows even and is the best method to use if the room is out of square or if you've chosen a tile with a definite pattern or design.

Locate the center point on each of two opposite walls, and snap a chalk line on the floor between the two points. Then find the centers of the other two walls and stretch your chalk line at right angles to the first line; snap this line only after you've used a carpenter's square to determine that the two lines cross at a precise right angle. If they don't, adjust the lines until they do.

Make a dry run before you actually set the tiles in adhesive. Lay one row of tiles along each working line, from the center of the room to each of two adjoining walls. Be sure to allow proper spacing for grout joints. Adjust your working lines as necessary to avoid very narrow border tiles.

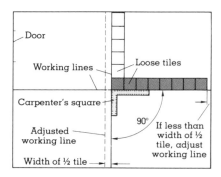

If you're working over a wood subfloor, temporarily nail batten boards along the two working lines that outline the quarter of the room farthest from the door; the battens will provide a rigid guide for the first row of tiles. (If you're working over a masonry subfloor, you'll have to use the chalk lines as your guides.) You'll set tiles using the sequence shown below, completing the floor quarter by quarter. Work on the quarter by the doorway last.

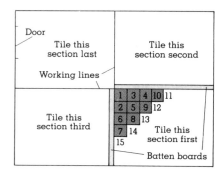

Set the tiles. Using a notched trowel, start spreading adhesive. Cover about a square yard at first, or the area you can comfortably tile before the adhesive begins to set.

Using a gentle twisting motion, place the first tile in the corner formed by the two battens (or chalk lines). With the same motion, place a second tile alongside the first. Continue laying tiles, following the sequence illustrated. Use molded plastic spacers to establish the proper width for the grout joints.

As the tiles are laid, set a piece of carpet-wrapped wood over them, and gently tap the wood with a mallet or hammer to "beat in" the tiles. Keep checking with a carpenter's square or straightedge to make sure each row is straight. Wiggle any stray tiles back into position.

To fit border tiles, measure each space carefully, subtract the width of two grout joints, and mark each tile for any necessary cuts.

When you complete the first quarter of the floor, remove the batten boards, then proceed with the next quarter. After all the tiles are placed, remove the spacers and clean the tile surface so it's completely free of adhesive.

Grout and seal the tile according to the instructions for wall tile on page 121.

Cabinets

In many homes, the need for bath-room storage has increased as people have collected more and more paraphernalia—bulky electric grooming appliances, children's bath toys, and cleaning supplies. For many families, a medicine cabinet just doesn't provide enough space.

This section will show you how to gain space by building a recessed storage cabinet between wall studs, or by adding a floor-mounted vanity cabinet.

For information on vanity cabinet styles, see page 33.

RECESSED CABINETS

One of the most economical and space-saving ways to add bathroom storage is to cut away the wall cover-ing between studs and install a re-cessed cabinet. Whether you want open shelves or a closed cabinet, you can gain extra space without sacrificing precious floor area.

When planning your cabinet, remember that its depth is limited by the depth of the wall studs; you may only be able to stack or hang items one deep inside the cabinet. Cabinet width, however, can vary: you can fit the cabinet between two adjacent studs or, for a wider stor-age area, place it between nonadja-cent studs, cutting out the interven-ing ones and framing the opening.

On these pages you'll learn how to build a recessed storage cabinet. First you'll draw a plan of the cabi-net to scale. Then you'll have to cut into the wall and perhaps frame an opening for the cabinet. Finally, you'll build and install the cabinet to your planned specifications.

If you elect to install a prefabri-cated cabinet, you'll use many of the same procedures. Read the manu-facturer's instructions for specific measurements and techniques.

Preparing the wall

This part of the project requires av-erage carpentry skills and careful attention to measurements.

Find the right wall. When you build a recessed cabinet between a pair of adjoining studs, you needn't be concerned about whether or not the wall is load-bearing. But if your planned cabinet is wider and you'll have to cut out one or more interven-ing studs, it's best to install it in a nonbearing wall (see pages 83–84)—unless you're an accomplished do-it-yourselfer, or you choose to hire a professional.

Before making a final decision on the location of your cabinet, check behind the wall for ob-structions such as wires, pipes, and ducts. You can do this by drilling small holes as follows.

First, shut off the electrical power to the bathroom by turning off circuit breakers or removing fuses. Use a test light to make sure all outlets are dead. Then, carefully drill or cut several small holes in the wall covering, spacing them widely over the area you plan to cut out. (Wall coverings such as tile, or panels of plastic, fiberglass, or wood cannot always be easily patched and may have to be replaced.)

Insert a length of wire in each hole, and move the wire around to see if it hits any obstructions such as wiring, plumbing, or heating ducts.

If you discover obstructions, you'll have to reroute them, or patch or replace the wall covering and find another suitable location. If the space under the wall covering is open, then move on to measuring and marking the outline of the stor-age cabinet on the wall.

Outline the cabinet. You may plan a cabinet to fit exactly between two wall studs, like that shown be-low. (Prefabricated units are usually made to fit that space.) You can also build a wider cabinet by cutting out studs. Once the studs are removed, you can build a cabinet to fill the entire space between the two outer studs, or add a new vertical framing piece to make the cabinet an inter-mediate width—say 1½ stud spaces wide (see illustrations on page 126).

To locate the studs (see page 84), either measure from a corner, knock on the wall until you hear a solid thud, or use a stud finder. Studs are usually 16 or 24 inches on center, so that the actual space available for a cabinet between two studs will be 14½ or 22½ inches.

When you've located the two studs nearest to the planned loca-tion of your cabinet's sides, find the studs' inside edges. (You'll cut away

BUILDING A CABINET BETWEEN TWO STUDS

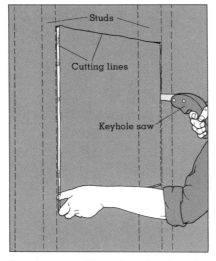

To cut away wallboard, scribe along the outline with a knife; cut with a keyhole saw while supporting cut wallboard.

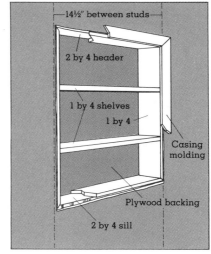

Install finished cabinet and nail sides to studs with finishing nails. Cover gap around edge with casing molding.

. . . Cabinets

the wall covering up to these edges.) Pierce gypsum wallboard with a finishing nail (or drill through plaster) until you find the edges. Then mark them by drawing vertical lines on the wall.

If the wall is tiled, you'll make a neater and easier job of it if you locate your lines along the grout lines between the tiles.

Mark the top and bottom edges of the cabinet outline with horizontal lines on the wall according to your plan, and check the lines for level. If you'll be cutting out studs, allow 1½ inches at top and bottom for installing a supporting header and sill (see illustration below).

Cut the wall covering. Once the outline is drawn on the wall, cut away the wall covering along the lines. Cut gypsum wallboard and panels of plastic, fiberglass, or wood with a keyhole saw. Carefully cut tile or plaster along the lines with a cold chisel and soft-headed steel hammer (protect your eyes); then cut the wallboard backing or lath and remove it.

Remove the studs. If you're building a cabinet wider than the distance between two studs, you'll cut out at least one intervening stud.

Use a hammer to remove any fireblocks connected to the stud. Then cut off the stud squarely with a handsaw along the top and bottom outlines. Move the cut-off section of the stud from side to side to free it from nails holding it to the wall covering in the room on the other side of the stud—take care not to damage that wall's finish.

Installing the cabinet

If your cabinet is designed to fit the space between two adjacent studs, skip over "Frame in the opening."

Frame in the opening. Add a header and sill for support where you cut out a stud. These can be single 2 by 4s in a nonbearing wall. (In a bearing wall, you'll need two 2 by 4s for the header.) To make a header and a sill for a nonbearing wall, cut 2 by 4s to fit in between the studs. Position the header and sill at top and bottom of the opening, and toenail their ends to the outside studs with 8-penny nails. Also nail through the header and sill into the ends of the cut-off studs above and below.

If your cabinet will be narrower than the exact width between studs, you'll have to frame the opening to

fit. Mark the outer edges of the cabinet's sides on the wall above and below the opening. Toenail vertical 2 by 4s to the header and sill, making sure they're plumb and that the inside edges are aligned with the marks. If 2 by 4s will be too thick to achieve the right-size opening, nail thinner lumber as required to the adjoining studs.

Build and install the cabinet. Once the wall framing is complete, construct the cabinet as shown in the illustration on page 125, modifying the design to fit your needs. First, build a shallow box, using plywood as the back and finished 1 by 4s for the sides, top, and bottom. Install metal or wood block shelf supports in the sides.

Position the cabinet between the studs and flush with the wall, then nail through the 1 by 4s with 6-penny finishing nails into the header, sill, and framing studs. Then add a casing molding around the cabinet wide enough to conceal the gap between the cabinet and the raw edges of the wall covering; miter the corners.

If you want doors on the cabinet, hinge them to the sides. Install shelves of wood or glass.

FRAMING FOR A CABINET WIDER THAN TWO STUDS

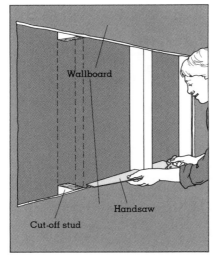

Mark and cut off in-between studs squarely with a handsaw to make room for wider cabinet.

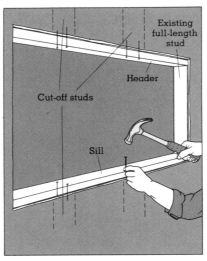

Frame opening top and bottom, nailing header and sill into cut-off and full-length studs.

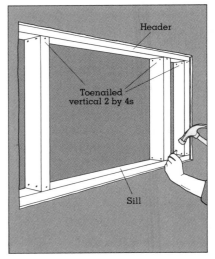

Toenail vertical 2 by 4s to header and sill for cabinets narrower than space between studs.

VANITY CABINETS

You can select a vanity cabinet to fit almost any style of bathroom. The vanity may be fitted with various types of countertops and sinks (see pages 32–33).

No matter what countertop and sink you prefer, the methods for removing and installing a prefabricated vanity cabinet in your bathroom are the same.

Before you buy a vanity cabinet, carefully measure the bathroom and note the placement of plumbing to be sure the new vanity will fit.

If a vanity cabinet higher than standard is more comfortable for the people in your household, add a frame of suitable height underneath the bottom before installing the cabinet.

Removing a vanity cabinet

To remove a plumbed vanity, you'll need to disconnect the plumbing and remove the sink and countertop (see page 98–99).

Pry away any vinyl wall base, floor covering, or molding from the base cabinet's kickspace or sides.

Old vanity cabinets are usually attached to wall studs with screws or nails through nailing strips at the back of each unit. Sometimes they're also fastened to the floor with nails through the kickspace trim or cabinet sides. Screws are easy to remove unless they're old and stripped. To remove nails, you may need to pry the cabinet away from the wall or floor with a prybar. To prevent damage, use a wood scrap between prybar and wall or floor. For a vanity with a solid back, you may have to shut off the water at the main valve and remove the sink shutoff valves to pull the vanity away from the wall.

Installing a vanity cabinet

You'll install the vanity cabinet first, then the countertop and sink.

Before you begin, remove any baseboard, moldings, or wall base

that might interfere. From the floor, measure up 34½ inches—the height of a standard vanity cabinet. Take several measurements and use the highest mark for your reference point. Draw a level line through the mark and across the wall.

If the vanity has a solid back, measure, mark, and cut the holes for the drain and water supply pipes, using a keyhole or saber saw.

For both solid and open-back vanities, locate and mark all wall studs (see page 84) in the wall above where the vanity will be installed. With helpers, if necessary, move the vanity into place.

Level the top of the vanity side-to-side and front-to-back, shimming between the vanity and floor as needed. Both shims and irregularities in the floor can be hidden by baseboard trim, vinyl wall base, or new flooring.

If the wall is irregular or not plumb, scribe and trim the back edges of the vanity's sides to fit the wall.

Some cabinets are designed with "scribing strips" along the sides—extra material you can shave down to achieve a perfect fit between the cabinet and an irregular wall.

To scribe a cabinet, first position it; then run a length of masking tape down the side to be scribed. Setting the points of a compass with pencil to the widest gap between the scribing strip and the wall, run the compass pivot down the wall next to the strip, as illustrated below. The wall's irregularities will be marked on the tape. Remove the vanity from the wall and use a block plane, file, or power belt sander to trim the scribing strip to the line. Then reinstall the cabinet.

If your cabinet doesn't have scribing strips, you can cover any large irregularities with decorative molding between the wall and cabinet.

When the cabinet is aligned with your reference marks on the wall, extend the stud location marks down to the hanger strip on the back of the vanity, drill pilot holes through the strip into the wall studs, and secure the vanity to the studs with woodscrews. If the studs aren't accessible, fasten the vanity to the wall with wall anchors.

Once the vanity cabinet is secure, install the countertop and sink, then connect the water supply lines, the trap, and the pop-up drain (see pages 99–101).

INSTALLING A VANITY CABINET

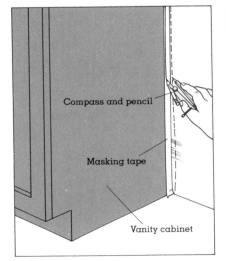

Compass and pencil

Masking tape

Vanity cabinet

Scribe and trim sides of vanity to make a snug fit when wall is out of plumb or is uneven.

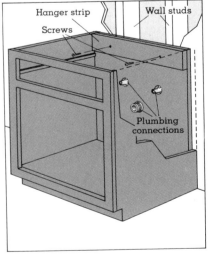

Hanger strip

Wall studs

Screws

Plumbing connections

Secure vanity cabinet to studs by screwing through hanger strip across the back. Drill pilot holes first.

Index